THE JUSTIFICATION READER

CLASSIC CHRISTIAN READERS

The Justification Reader

FORTHCOMING VOLUMES

The Good Works Reader

THE JUSTIFICATION READER

Thomas C. Oden

WILLIAM B. EERDMANS PUBLISHING COMPANY
GRAND RAPIDS, MICHIGAN / CAMBRIDGE, U.K.

Wm. B. Eerdmans Publishing Co.
255 Jefferson Ave. S.E., Grand Rapids, Michigan 49503 /
P.O. Box 163, Cambridge CB3 9PU U.K.
www.eerdmans.com

Printed in the United States of America

07 06 05 04 03 02   7 6 5 4 3 2 1

ISBN 0-8028-3966-5

Unless otherwise noted, patristic quotations derive from the Ancient Christian
Commentary on Scripture, reprinted by permission of InterVarsity Press.

Contents

CONTENTS

PART TWO

GRACE ALONE

CHAPTER ONE

Why Imputed Grace Dislodges All Boasting

PART THREE

BY FAITH ALONE

Abbreviations

ACCS	T. C. Oden, ed. *Ancient Christian Commentary on Scripture*. 11 vols. to date. Downers Grove, Ill.: InterVarsity Press, 1998-.
ACW	J. Quasten et al., eds. *Ancient Christian Writers: The Works of the Fathers in Translation*. 55 vols. New York: Paulist Press, 1946-.
ad loc.	Latin "to the place"; here cites a source ordered by scriptural chapter and verse, usually referring the reader to the page on which the Scripture text in question is discussed.
AEG	H. D. Smith, ed. *Ante-Nicene Exegesis of the Gospels*. 6 vols. London: SPCK, 1925.
ANF	A. Roberts and J. Donaldson, eds. *Ante-Nicene Fathers*. American reprint of the Edinburgh edition. 10 vols. Buffalo, N.Y.: Christian Literature, 1885-1896. Reprint, Grand Rapids: Eerdmans, 1951-1956. Reprint, 1978-1980.
BCP	*Book of Common Prayer* (1662). Royal Breviar's edition. London: SPCK, n.d.
BOC	T. G. Tappert, ed. *The Book of Concord* (1580). Philadelphia: Muhlenberg Press, 1959.
BT	*Bibliotheca Scriptorum Graecorum et Romanorum Teubneriana*. Leipzig: Teubner, 1864-1939.
Calvin Comm.	John Calvin. J. King, trans. *Commentaries*. 45 vol. in 22. Edinburgh: Calvin Translation Society, 1845-1856. Reprint, Grand Rapids: Baker, 1981.
Catech.	Catechism or Catechetical
CC	J. Leith, ed. *Creeds of the Churches*. Richmond, Va.: John Knox Press, 1979.
CCL	*Corpus Christianorum. Series Latina*. 175+ vols. to date. Turnhout [Belgium]: Brepols, 1954-.

CD	Karl Barth. G. W. Bromiley et al., eds. *Church Dogmatics.* 4 vols. Edinburgh: T. & T. Clark, 1936-1969.
CEC	J. A. Cramer, ed. *Catena in Epistolas Catholicas.* Vol. 8 of *Catenae Graecorum Patrum in Novum Testamentum.* Oxford: E. Typographeo Academico, 1840.
CER	Origen. T. Heither, ed. *Commentarii in Epistulam ad Romanos* (Commentary on the Epistle to the Romans). 5 vols. Freiburg im Breisgau: Herder, 1990-1995.
CGPEP	J. A. Cramer, ed. *Catenae in Sancti Pauli Epistolas ad Galatas, Ephesios, Philippenses, Colossenses, Thessalonicenses.* Vol. 6 of *Catenae Graecorum Patrum in Novum Testamentum.* Oxford: E. Typographeo Academico, 1842.
COC	P. Schaff, ed. *Creeds of Christendom.* 3 vols. New York: Harper and Bros., 1919.
Comm.	Commentary
Conf.	Confessions
CPE	Theodoret. C. Marriott, ed. *Commentarius in Omnes B. Pauli Epistolas.* 2 vols. Oxford: J. H. Parker, 1852-1870.
CR	Ulrich Zwingli, John Calvin, and Philipp Melanchthon. K. G. Bretschneider et al., eds. *Corpus Reformatorum (Huldreich Zwingli Sämtliche Werke; Johannis Calvini Opera; Philippi Melanchthonis Opera).* 99 vols. Berlin: C. A. Schwetschke and Leipzig: Heinsius, 1834-1905.
CSEL	*Corpus Scriptorum Ecclesiasticorum Latinorum.* 90+ vols. Vienna: Hoelder-Pichler-Tempsky, 1866-.
DER	Gerald Bray, ed. *Documents of the English Reformation.* Minneapolis: Fortress Press, 1994.
DSWT	Thomas C. Oden. *Doctrinal Standards in the Wesleyan Tradition.* Grand Rapids: Francis Asbury Press, 1988.
DT	Joseph Pohle. A. Preuss, ed. *Dogmatic Theology.* 12 vols. St. Louis: B. Herder, 1922.
ECW	M. Staniforth, trans. *Early Christian Writers: The Apostolic Fathers.* London: Penguin Books, 1968.
ENPK	H. J. Frede, ed. *Ein neuer Paulustext und Kommentar* (A New Pauline Text and Commentary). 2 vols. Vols. 7-8 of *Vetus Latina.* Freiburg im Breisgau: Herder, 1974.
F&T	Søren Kierkegaard. W. Lowrie, trans. *Fear and Trembling and Sickness Unto Death.* Princeton: Princeton University Press, 1968.
FC	R. J. Deferrari, ed. *Fathers of the Church: A New Translation.* 100+ vols. to date. Washington, D.C.: Catholic University of America Press, 1947-.

FEF	W. A. Jurgens, ed. *The Faith of the Early Fathers*. 3 vols. Collegeville, Minn.: Liturgical Press, 1970-79.
FGG	Gregory of Nyssa. H. Musurillo, trans. *From Glory to Glory: Texts from Gregory of Nyssa's Mystical Writings*. Crestwood, N.Y.: St. Vladimir's Seminary Press, 1979.
FGNK	T. Zahn, ed. *Forschungen zur Geschichte des neutestamentlichen Kanons*. 10 vols. Erlangen: A. Deichart, 1881-1929.
GJC	*The Gospel of Jesus Christ: An Evangelical Celebration*. In: J. N. Akers et al., eds. *This We Believe: The Good News of Jesus Christ for the World*. Grand Rapids: Zondervan, 2000.
Hom.	Homilies or Homily
Inst.	John Calvin. *Institutes of the Christian Religion*. LCC, vols. 20, 21.
IOEP	John Chrysostom. F. Field, ed. *Interpretatio omnium Epistolarum Paulinarum per Homilias Facta*. 7 vols. Oxford: J. H. Parker, 1845-1862.
JD	Lutheran World Federation and the Roman Catholic Church. *Joint Declaration on the Doctrine of Justification*. Grand Rapids: Eerdmans, 2000.
JJW	John Wesley. N. Curnock, ed. *The Journal of the Reverend John Wesley*. 8 vols. London: Epworth, 1909-1916.
JThS	Journal of Theological Studies.
KG	Alexander B. Bruce. *The Kingdom of God*. 6th edition. Edinburgh: T. & T. Clark, 1909.
KJV	King James Version (1611)
LCC	J. Baillie et al., eds. *The Library of Christian Classics*. 26 vols. Philadelphia: Westminster, 1953-1966.
LW	Martin Luther. J. J. Pelikan and H. T. Lehmann, eds. *Luther's Works*. 55 vols. St. Louis: Concordia, 1955-1976.
LXX	Septuagint
MLS	Martin Luther. J. Dillenberger, ed. *Martin Luther: Selections From His Writings*. New York: Doubleday, 1961.
NEB	New English Bible (1970)
NPNF	P. Schaff et al., eds. *A Select Library of the Nicene and Post-Nicene Fathers of the Christian Church*, Series 1 and 2 (14 vols. each). Buffalo, N.Y.: Christian Literature, 1887-1894. Reprint, Edinburgh: T. & T. Clark, and Grand Rapids: Eerdmans, 1952-1956. Reprint, 1971-1979.
NT	New Testament
NTA 15	K. Staab, ed. *Pauluskommentare aus der griechischen Kirche: Aus Katenenhandschriften gesammelt und herausgegeben* (Pauline Commentary from the Greek Church: Collected and Edited from

	Catena Writings). Neutestamentliche Abhandlungen 15. Münster in Westfalen: Aschendorff, 1933.
NUNT	John Wesley. *Explanatory Notes upon the New Testament.* Reprint, Naperville, Ill.: Allenson, 1958.
OF	John of Damascus. *On the Orthodox Faith.* NPNF 2 IX; FC 37.
OOT	Archibald A. Hodge. *Outlines of Theology.* Reprint of rewritten and enlarged edition of 1878. Grand Rapids: Eerdmans, 1928.
Orat.	Oration or orations
PG	J.-P. Migne, ed. *Patrologia Graeca.* 166 vols. Paris: Migne, 1857-1886.
PL	J.-P. Migne, ed. *Patrologia Latina.* 221 vols. Paris: Migne, 1844-1864.
PL *Supp.*	A. Hamman, ed. *Patrologiae Latinae Supplementum.* 5 vols. in 6. Paris: Garnier Frères, 1958-1974.
SCD	H. Denzinger, ed. R. J. Deferrari, trans. *Sources of Catholic Dogma (Enchiridion Symbolorum).* St. Louis: Herder, 1957.
SCF	Henry E. Jacobs. *A Summary of the Christian Faith.* Philadelphia: General Council Publication House, 1905.
SHD	Reinhold Seeberg. C. E. Hay, trans. *Text-book of the History of Doctrines.* Reprint of rev. edition of 1905. 2 vols. in 1. Grand Rapids: Baker, 1952.
ST	(1) Thomas Aquinas. English Dominican Fathers, eds. *Summa Theologica.* 1st complete American edition. 3 vols. New York: Benziger, 1947. (2) S. Gamertsfelder. *Systematic Theology.* Cleveland: C. Hauser, 1913. Reprint, Harrisburg, Pa.: Evangelical Publishing House, 1952. (3) A. H. Strong. *Systematic Theology.* Old Tappan, N.J.: Revell, 1907. Reprint, 1979.
SW	John Calvin. J. Dillenberger, ed. *John Calvin: Selections from His Writings.* Missoula, Mont.: Scholar's Press, 1975.
TDNT	Gerhard Kittel et al. G. W. Bromiley, ed. *Theological Dictionary of the New Testament.* Abridged in 1 vol. Grand Rapids: Eerdmans, 1985.
Tho. Aq.	Thomas Aquinas
TNC	Martin Chemnitz. J. A. O. Preuss, trans. *The Two Natures in Christ.* St. Louis: Concordia, 1971.
Trent	H. J. Schroeder, trans. *The Canons and Decrees of the Council of Trent.* St. Louis: B. Herder, 1941. Reprint, Rockford, Ill.: TAN, 1978.
VELKD	Position Paper of the Joint Committee of the United Evangelical Lutheran Church of Germany and the LWF German National Committee regarding the document "The Condemnations of the Reformation Era. Do They Still Divide?" In: *Lehrverurteilungen im Gespräch.* Göttingen: Vandenhoeck & Ruprecht, 1993.
WA	Martin Luther. *D. Martin Luthers Werke.* Kritische Gesamtausgabe (Weimarer Ausgabe). Weimar: H. Böhlau, 1883-.

WJO — John Owen. W. H. Goold, ed. *The Works of John Owen.* 17 vols. [N.p.]: Johnstone & Hunter, 1850-1853. Reprint, 16 vols., Edinburgh and Carlisle, Pa.: Banner of Truth Trust, 1965-68.

WJW — John Wesley. T. Jackson, ed. *Works of the Rev. John Wesley.* 14 vols. London: Wesleyan Conference Office, 1872.

WJWB — John Wesley. F. Baker, ed. *The Works of John Wesley.* Bicentennial edition. 23 vols. Nashville: Abingdon, 1984- (formerly pub. by Oxford University Press).

WLS — Martin Luther. E. Plass, ed. *What Luther Says.* 3 vols. St. Louis: Concordia, 1959.

WNB — John Wesley. T. C. Oden, ed. *The New Birth.* San Francisco: Harper & Row, 1984.

Introduction

1. The Promise

My purpose is plainly to set forth nothing more or less than the classic Christian teaching of salvation by grace through faith, and only those parts of that teaching on which there is substantial agreement between traditions of East and West, Catholic, Protestant, and Orthodox, including charismatic and Pentecostal teaching.

I promise to make no new contribution to theology. I will not set before you anything new or innovative. This is not an attempt at comedy. I only hope that my own personal voice does not drown out the magnificent voices of the Apostles, the Evangelists, Athanasius, John Chrysostom, Augustine, Luther, Calvin, and Wesley. As a former addict of fad theology, I have come home to ancient ecumenical Christianity. My only desire is to give voice to the truth of the early apostolic tradition without change or distortion. If something here should inadvertently seem to be new, it would be a decisive lapse from my intention.

If you are not a Christian, there is still much to learn from such an exercise. Take it as an act of empathy — on the premise that your Christian friends believe in what they call justification by grace through faith. Suppose you engage in an empathic exercise asking: How can I put myself in their shoes for an evening of reading and understand them better?

Or if you prefer, you have permission to think of this purely as a historical exercise: What have Christians of all times believed about salvation, regardless of what I might believe? But be forewarned that it might change your life.

This book is mostly for those who already relish the true taste of the early apostolic tradition as freshly remembered in its first five centuries. You may already know how to recognize its voices. If so you will not mind investing time listening to God speak through these earliest interpreters of the written Word. You have taste buds; you are already salivating.

So: What do Christians of all times and places believe about justification by grace through faith? Is there a stable, central core of substantial agreement? This collection of classic writings mostly of the earliest Christian centuries shows what that core is. It is intended for the faithful lay reader who wants to understand what Christians traditionally believe about God's saving act as taught by the consensus of earliest scripture interpreters. Whether one agrees with that consensus or not, the task is to identify it.

Such an exercise must be a meditation on the whole range of the Bible concerning a single theme of it: justification, the heart of the gospel. The three parts of this teaching have a simple organization, based on Ephesians 2:8:

- Salvation
- By Grace
- Through Faith

2. The Heart of the Gospel

Some may think it daunting to face texts written 1500 or more years ago. But the blessing to be received is profound. I promise you that if you read these explanations carefully, you will for the rest of your life understand the heart of the gospel. In the few hours it will take you to read this, your heart and mind will be bathed in the saving Word of God in an unforgettable way.

Until the believer has rightly understood what Scripture teaches on this "uprighting" or "justifying" act of God, one is likely to remain confused by much else that the New Testament teaches.

A. The Special Comfort of God's Free Grace

Classic Christian teaching speaks often of the exceeding comfort of God's justifying grace.

1. The Unique Blessing of Justification

Those who come to God come only by grace — only through trusting wholly in what God has already accomplished on the cross.

No Christian teaching is more crucial to peace of conscience than justification. The central blessing of Christian living hinges upon the proper understanding of the free grace of the sovereign God (Calvin, Inst. 3.11). Rightly believed, it consecrates all other energies of the redeemed person and community.

Salvation by grace through faith is itself the central blessing that most distinctively belongs to life in Christ. Who is most completely freed to live a truly blessed life? One "whose transgressions are forgiven, whose sins are covered. Blessed is the one whose sin the Lord does not count against him and in whose spirit is no deceit" (Ps. 32:1-2). If you are one whose sin the Lord does not count against you, you are blessed in the distinctive way that believers are blessed. Your life is not trapped in the deceit that comes from defensive self-justification.

This faith has often prompted astonishing courage — exceptionally fearless responses from those who put their lives on the line in confessing it. You belong to a history of women and men in whom such intrepid heroism has often been put to test and lived out. These were ordinary people from whom dauntless acts might otherwise not have been expected. They displayed extraordinary courage and peace of conscience even amid martyrdom. Do not forget the history of martyrdom as you read this testimony. It has been bled for.

2. Basic Definitions

The nature of justification is pardon, its sole condition is faith, its sole ground is the righteousness of God, and its fruits and evidences are good works.

3

For Protestants, the most common definition is stated in the Augsburg Confession: "It is also taught among us that we cannot obtain forgiveness of sin and righteousness before God by our own merits, works, or satisfactions, but that we receive forgiveness of sin and become righteous before God by grace, for Christ's sake, through faith, when we believe that Christ suffered for us and that for his sake our sin is forgiven, and righteousness and eternal life are given to us. For God will regard and reckon this faith as righteousness, as Paul says in Romans 3:21-26 and 4:5."[1]

Why is it so important to our happiness that we understand rightly an undeceitful, guileless, uprighted relation with God?

B. The Centrality of Justification in Christian Teaching

1. The Decisive Baseline of Evangelical Teaching

Luther regarded justification as the "ruler and judge over all other Christian doctrines."[2] Of justification he wrote: "Nothing in this article can be given up or compromised. . . . On this article rests all that we teach. . . . Therefore we must be quite certain and have no doubts about it. Otherwise all is lost."[3]

Justification is central to the Christian teaching of salvation. All who affirm classic Christian teaching, whether charismatic or Catholic or Orthodox or Baptist, embrace this teaching. So pivotal is it to Christian preaching that if unbalanced in any way, reverberations are felt in the whole edifice of faith. Misleading pitfalls must be avoided if we are to believe this word and teach it wisely.

What most informed lay Protestants of the eighteenth century knew fairly well concerning justification, few grasp profoundly in our generation. These times call us to return to the basics, to this central baseline of Christian teaching, and especially to its greatest classic teachers — not only Luther and Calvin, but the earliest New Testament interpreters like Irenaeus and Athanasius.

Catholics have recently agreed with Lutherans in their "Joint Decla-

---

1. CC, p. 69.
2. WA 39, I, 205.
3. Smalcald Articles, II.1, BOC, p. 292.

4

ration" that justification "is more than just one part of Christian doctrine. It stands in an essential relation to all truths of faith, which are to be seen as internally related to each other. It is an indispensable criterion that constantly serves to orient all the teaching and practice of our churches to Christ. When Lutherans emphasize the unique significance of this criterion, they do not deny the interrelation and significance of all truths of faith. When Catholics see themselves as bound by several criteria, they do not deny the special function of the message of justification" (JD 16). Both have solemnly agreed that justification is "the touchstone for testing at all times whether a particular interpretation of our relation to God can claim the name 'Christian'" (JD 3.18). But much wrestling is needed to grasp these implications.

2. Why Is It a Comforting Doctrine?

Luther taught that every time you insist that I am a sinner, just so often do you call me to remember the benefit of Christ my Redeemer, upon whose shoulders, and not upon mine, lie all my sins. So, when you say that I am a sinner, you do not terrify, but comfort me immeasurably.

Justification "brings us into a state of most blessed peace and favor with God, and secures every other blessing needful for time and eternity" (New Hampshire Baptist Confession, 1833, Article V).[4]

The Anglican Articles of Religion underscored the special comfort and benefit of justification teaching: "We are accounted righteous before God, only for the merit of our Lord and Savior Jesus Christ by faith, and not for our own works or deservings. Therefore, that we are justified by faith only is a most wholesome doctrine, and very full of comfort" (Thirty-Nine Articles, Art. XI).[5]

---

4. Of Justification, COC 3:744.

5. BCP; Of the Justification of Man. This article is identical with Article IX of the Methodist Twenty-five Articles of Religion. Similar language is found in the Heidelberg Catechism, Article 1, COC 3:307-8.

3. The Limits of Our Powers of Restitution

What is the problem to which justification is an answer? In a word *sin*, which estranges us from God's holiness.

Why can't we forgive ourselves?

No one can go back and undo all that one has wrongly or harmfully done. None of my efforts at restitution, however sincere and serious, can ever be fully adequate to the sufferings I have caused. No payment will suffice for a damage that has ongoing and unpredictable consequences to the next generation. I cannot stop the chain of effects caused by my previous mistakes and sins. If it were possible for me to provide a complete and absolute restitution for all those wrongs I have done to others, then I might imagine that the grace of divine pardon would be made somehow less necessary. But this is not possible.

This fact is especially poignant in the case of the taking of life. Once taken, a life can never be given back again. No restitution is possible. This stark fact is a part of the deep struggle of conscience in the case of the syndrome of post-abortion depression. However repentant one may be, the life taken cannot be given back. But the taking of life is only one example of the limits of personal restitution. No one can halt the sequence of effects caused by sexual abuse or of violence done to children.

All sin has the character of setting chains of consequences in motion that cannot be simply backtracked or reversed. No simple restitution can ever be made for sexual infidelity to one's covenant partner, since a solemn inviolable promise once broken is forever broken. Only God's gift of forgiveness is able to overcome this alienation, so destructive to children and family integrity. We have all caused harm that can never be made up for by human hands or works. This is why we stand in such dire need of justification by grace.

C. Why a Justification Reader?

This Reader is the first of a series on key themes of classic Christianity that remain pertinent, even urgent, today.

1. *It Provides a Model for Classic Christian Reasoning*

This Reader provides a pattern for lay persons for thinking with the historic communion of saints about a particularly decisive point of Christian teaching. It shows how genuine Christian teaching is consistently based on Scripture, especially as understood by its most reliable classic interpreters, those most widely trusted by the historic circle of believers of all generations. It sets forth the classic method of Christian reasoning.

Anyone can reason this way. It is not meant for clergy only. Any lay person can think with the whole church about the whole of Scripture, and validate its meaning within his own conscience through the guidance of the Holy Spirit. This classic method is not intimidating and is easily accessible to all. It hinges on comparing scriptural texts.

It is regrettable that so much contemporary theology has largely forgotten how to think this way. This method was unwisely discarded several decades ago, except among a few. The result is that in our time we do not even have many of these patristic texts readily accessible to us in any modern language for exercising this classic approach in the search for truth. Doctrinally we remain text-deprived, Scripture-hungry, argument-deficient.

2. *Why Is Justification Teaching Especially Pertinent Today?*

Of all the topics we might have taken up to inaugurate this series, and set forth this way of thinking about Christian teaching, why justification? Three reasons:

- Justification is easily misunderstood, but its misunderstandings easily corrected.
- It is crucial to salvation in all Christian traditions.
- It remains a stumbling block to the unity of the body of Christ, due to its different histories of interpretation over the last thousand years.

If we can grasp and articulate the classic basis for thinking about the faith that is to some real but imperfect extent shared (despite all other cultural differences) between Orthodox, Protestants, and Catholics on justification, one of the major reasons for our historic divisions will to that extent be undercut. It is ironic that justification is one of the doctrines that has most divided Christians since the sixteenth century. This is why this topic comes first in this series.

3. Simplicity

My passion is for simple, straightforward classic teaching. I will use common contemporary English in presenting ideas and texts that have sometimes been burdened with old-fashioned expressions. I will try to remove obsolete language without tilting the substance of the meaning or cheap paraphrasing.

The languages and cultures in which this teaching emerged and developed were extremely varied: Jewish, Greco-Roman, North African, Byzantine, medieval, Reformation, and modern. Though expressed differently, the core of the teaching is cohesive. This Reader seeks to simplify the lay person's access to these teachings by providing a "dynamic equivalency" translation in common, current English idioms.

I solicit your prayers that my work and your reading will be accompanied by the Holy Spirit in order that the apostolic faith will be rightly preserved without addition or distortion. I remain entirely dedicated to unoriginality. Nothing I know is more profoundly relevant to the modern condition.

4. On the Genre of the "Reader"

This book is a Reader. This means it presents readings, especially from authoritative classic sources, woven into a reasoned argument. It limits its range of questions to this single momentous issue: What does it mean to be justified by grace through faith?

The classic sources found in this Reader are focused primarily on two historical periods: the church fathers and the Reformation. Only a few modern sources are occasionally referenced, in order to reinforce the point that this teaching is shared by all Christians of all times.

I have you alone — the living, breathing actual reader — as the sole person in mind to whom I wish to convey these treasures. I want you to understand every sentence. I pray for you to understand what I write in the same way that I understand it, but more so as Christians everywhere and always have understood it. When I fail to convey that classic meaning sharply and rightly, I pray that you may not be misled, that my misjudgments will soon be corrected by what I later say.

This is a Lay Reader. It does not pretend to be a detailed technical commentary on all of its excerpts. Its aim is economy. Its task is not to place each text in its historical, social, political context — that obviously would require a shelf of books instead of a single book. I intend to give you the heart and gist of classic Christian salvation teaching without any unnecessary scholarly flourishes or pretenses. If you want a detailed discussion of the historical or social context of these texts, you have the wrong book in hand. This one is intended for anyone who is hungry for the Word.

Some purists may question any effort at excerpting. If so, ask yourself whether you ever make use of anthologies or collections of primary sources. Surely collections of poetry are not to be thrown out of your library. Anyone who reads poetry reads carefully culled excerpts of a poet's larger work. This Reader is more analogous to a poetry collection than to a sociological or philosophical explanation. If you love poetry, you do not demean the work of careful text selection in the design of anthologies and primary source collections.[6]

6. A comparative bibliographical note on the genre of "the Reader": The pattern I am following is similar in intent to several other classic works: Henry Bettenson's *Documents of the Christian Church* (London: Oxford University Press, 1963); J. Stevenson's *Creeds, Councils and Controversies: Documents Illustrating the History of the Church, A.D. 337-461* (London: SPCK, 1966); John H. Leith's *Creeds of the Churches* (Atlanta: John Knox, 3rd ed. 1982); and W. A. Jurgens's *The Faith of the Early Fathers*, 3 vols. (Collegeville, Minn.: Liturgical Press, 1970-1979). What makes it different is that all of the above are organized chronologically whereas this Reader is organized thematically by a sequential order of topics. For comparable examples of the genre, see my four-volume edition of *Classical Pastoral Care* (Grand Rapids: Baker, 3rd ed. 2000); *The Handbook of Public Prayer*, ed. Roger Geffen (New York: Macmillan, 1963); and the *Treasury of the Christian Faith: An Encyclopedic Handbook of the Range and Witness of Christianity*, ed. Stanley I. Stuber and Thomas Clark (New York: Association Press, 1949). My Reader is not, however, like many standard non-contextualizing books of quotations, such as Frank S. Mead's massive *Encyclopedia of Religious Quotations* (London: Peter Davies, 1965), because this series organizes and discusses these primary source selections into a sequential argument and narrative. It would be more comparable to Frank W. Magill, *Magill's Quotations in Context* (New York: Harper and Row, 1965), but it is not organized as an alphabetical list of quotations arranged according to key words, as in Magill. Rather, the selections are embedded within a sequential flow of argument touching

5. Why Have These Texts Remained Shockingly Inaccessible Elsewhere?

It is a sad fact that we have not had sufficient access to the classical sources that discuss justification. We remain densely unprepared for solid argument on this theme. Why? Many of the early church sources that were available in Greek and Latin to Luther, Calvin, and Wesley have remained untranslated into English for several centuries. We are here providing many of them. But why have they been ignored, especially on such a pivotal subject?

It is a familiar assumption of many modern Protestant laity and clergy that the classical writers of the first millennium knew little or nothing of justification by grace through faith as understood by Paul, Luther, Calvin, and the Reformation. This is a distorted assumption shared ironically by both modern liberal Protestants and modern evangelical Protestants. This misconception is seldom found in classic sixteenth-century Reformation writers, but it is an especially characteristic conjecture of liberal Protestants since Harnack, who constantly belittled the gross accommodations of patristic writers to Hellenization and Greek philosophy. Luther himself, of course, knew better.

---

upon most key points on the classic Christian teaching of justification. The genre is similar in intent to *An Aquinas Reader,* ed. Mary T. Clark (New York: Doubleday, 1972), except it does not focus on a single writer, but rather on a single question. It is even more similar to *Anglicanism: The Thought and Practice of the Church of England, Illustrated from the Religious Literature of the Seventeenth Century,* ed. Paul Elmer More and Frank Leslie Cross (London: SPCK, 1962), but it spans primarily the early centuries, and all communions. It is something like *Classics of Protestantism,* ed. Vergilius Ferm (New York: Philosophical Library, 1959), but is organized systematically, not chronologically. It is more akin in its narrative style to S. W. Duffield's *English Hymns: Their Authors and History* (New York: Funk and Wagnalls, 1886), than it is to *The Concise Oxford Dictionary of Proverbs,* ed. John Simpson (New York: Oxford University Press, 1993), or to *The International Dictionary of Thoughts: An Encyclopedia of Quotations from Every Age,* compiled by J. P. Bradley, L. F. Daniels, and T. C. Jones (Chicago: Ferguson, 1969). Its audience is comparable in some ways to that of J. Robert Wright's *Readings for the Daily Office from the Early Church* (New York: Church Hymnal Corporation, 1991). The genre is more like A. Cohen's *Everyman's Talmud* (New York: Schocken, 1949) or the *Hasidic Anthology,* ed. Louis Newman (New York: Schocken, 1963) than Adin Steinsaltz's *The Essential Talmud* (New York: Basic Books, 1976).

6. A Welcoming Note for Orthodox and Catholic Readers

Although this Reader is published by a Protestant press that seeks an ecumenical audience, it might have seemed more fitting if it had been published simultaneously by a Protestant and a Catholic press (or Orthodox), had that been feasible. Although the subject deserves and hopes for both Catholic and Orthodox readers, I recognize that religious publishing is as divided as the religious traditions themselves. Joint publication is more than one can expect, though not more than one can pray for. I therefore present this through a Protestant press, hoping that by some work of providence it will also be found in due course and read by Catholics and Orthodox, since its patristic sources are equally treasured by all classic Catholic and Orthodox Christians.

PART ONE

JUSTIFICATION

The Ancient Fathers
on Evangelical Justification

The quickest route to the rediscovery of the unity of the body of Christ is the rediscovery of ancient Christian texts that express that unity, especially texts prior to Christianity's tragic divisions. They remain the patrimony of all Christians today of all continents and races and cultures. These texts are the Fathers of the Church, the consensus-bearing teachers of the earliest Christian centuries, who stood under the authority of the written word.

A. Typical Misconceptions of Classic
Christian Teaching on Saving Faith

The justification teaching of the ancient Christian writers is neglected. While Protestants often complain that Catholics missed the point entirely, Catholics tend to ignore the Protestant complaint. Meanwhile the Orthodox are sure that the only way to get things right is for everyone to come home to Orthodoxy, whether Greek, Russian, Coptic, or Syriac.

1. Peacemaking among the Divided Faithful

The idea that the ancient Christian fathers and mothers all terribly misunderstood salvation by faith (the faith they were willing to die for) is itself an incorrect and mischievous modern misconception.

The idea that in the long centuries between Paul and Luther no one but Protestants (and only a few of them) rightly understood justification is itself an intemperate idea, and neglectful, I think, of many ancient consensus-bearing texts.

Equally ironic is the fact that many Catholic and Orthodox laity and clergy remain unaware that key aspects of their own liturgy are congruent with many aspects of classic Protestant teaching of salvation by faith.

What follows is a peacemaking effort between Protestants, Orthodox, and Catholics on salvation teaching based on a simple presentation and comparison of doctrinal texts widely recognized as official church teaching or expositions of representative orthodox voices in widely different Christian cultures and communions. My effort is to show a worldwide consensus on salvation teaching among two thousand years of Christians of extremely varied historical and cultural memories.

2. My Simple Thesis

My thesis: There is indeed a textually defined consensual classic Christian teaching on salvation by grace through faith. This can be demonstrated textually by presenting the evidences of consensual interpretation in the classic exposition of those key biblical texts upon which all agree that a Christian doctrine of justification must be grounded. So what follows is a highly textual evidentiary presentation.

My intent is simple: I will show how the classic Christian exegetes, mostly of the first five centuries, dealt with Paul's justification teaching. In doing so I will ask whether there is already formed in the first millennium a reliable, clear, central core of the classic Christian teaching of salvation by grace through faith.

Note that I am not approaching the question deductively by attempting first to define what the Christian teaching of salvation is, and only then to see if that teaching is indeed found in scripture and consensual scriptural interpretation.

Rather, I proceed inductively to discern what the earliest Christian scriptural commentators in fact explicitly wrote about precisely these key salvation texts of the written Word read every Sunday in churches everywhere. When I say "everywhere," I mean everywhere the church exists or has existed in any century. For there has never been any doubt about the

canonical status of Paul's letters, to which most of these patristic reflec-
tions appear as a commentary.

By this means I will ask whether there is indeed an orthodox consensual Christian teaching of salvation to which Protestants, Catholics, Orthodox, charismatics, and Pentecostals can all confidently appeal, without
denying their different historical memories. All these traditions are free to
claim legitimate ownership of their own patrimony, to honor and cherish
and celebrate these pre-European, pre-modern, pre-medieval classic exegetes of scripture, who wrote long before Orthodox, Catholics, and Protestants began quarreling. These quarrels did not develop until close to the
end of the first millennium.

3. Why the Classic Christian Consensus Is Not Properly Described as Either European or Western

Millions of Christians in Africa and Asia are looking toward pre-European
exegesis to guide them in fresh, sound, plausible ways to insights not dominated by corrupted post-colonial modern western premises. The church
Fathers are pre-European.

By pre-European I mean before Charlemagne, during most of the
first half of the first millennium when most of what we today call Europe
(especially northern Europe, apart from the Mediterranean coast) was
largely without a distinguished written culture, not yet having a cohesive
cultural entity or literary tradition. Remember that Beowulf was not written down until the eighth century.

Note that classical Christian teaching does not appeal to early consensual exegesis on the modern democratic premise that a majority of
scholars or exegetes might vote up or down in a particular way. It is rather
the whole church, the worshiping community worldwide, deciding and
freely consenting over many generations, rather than particular scholars.
Classic Christian scholarship is validated by lay consent only when it reflects the previously received consensus of apostolic teaching in the worshiping communities.

General ecumenical consent proceeds on the premise that the whole
church is being actively guided by the Holy Spirit into all truth amid the
hazards of history. This providence is especially validated when apostolic
truth is on trial, and especially where martyrdom is evident. All classic

Christian exegetes from Ignatius and Irenaeus through Eusebius to Augustine were confident of that providential guidance. The exegetes most widely remembered and received by Christians of many different languages and cultural assumptions are those whose writings were most carefully preserved by the church — of both East and West — against all odds and amid numerous persecutions. These are assumed in this worldwide, transgenerational *communio sanctorum* to be indeed the most dependable guides to the witness of the Holy Spirit to the truth of the gospel.

4. Why This Presentation of Evidence Is So Urgently Needed amid Uncharitable Polemics among Evangelicals, Liberals, Catholics, and Orthodox Today

There is the deep and urgent hunger among many believing Evangelicals, Orthodox, and Catholics for rediscovering the unity of the body of Christ. This yearning is accompanied by a gnawing sense of disappointment with the actual useful outcomes of modern historicist scriptural studies, tilted as they are toward the reductionist philosophy of naturalism.

There is an emerging post-critical evangelical awareness that vital preaching and mission must now go beyond the speculative imagination of the faith-aversive biblical critics of recent decades. Meanwhile the models and examples of ancient exegesis remain shockingly unfamiliar to modern pastors and unfairly caricatured by avant-garde biblical scholars who have not yet bothered to read much of the Fathers, although they are beginning to do so. The Fathers were not ignored by Calvin, Chemnitz, Wesley, or Edwards, who easily read Greek, Latin, and Hebrew. But they are largely ignored today, and many of the most important sources have remained untranslated into modern languages. This situation cries out for honest brokers between ancient sources and modern lay readers. This disaster would not have occurred if we had kept Latin and Greek in the school curriculum.

In this arena, novelty is just as addictive for avant-garde evangelicals as it is for liberals nurtured by and still belatedly feeding upon modernity's tired illusions. Optimistic fantasies about cheap grace, as if unaccompanied by any serious history of sin, are especially tempted to fall into these familiar ideological traps of humanistic faddism. As a former addict to novelty, I plead that evangelicals might turn away from the temptation of compulsive exegetical faddism. Philosophical and critical fads are like dope for those modernizing junkies (including some evangelicals and Catholics) who are trying to accommodate to a dying modernity and to validate their credentials within a morose university ethos.

5. How Both Evangelical and Liberal Assumptions Have Tilted the Perception of Ancient Orthodox Christian Salvation Teaching

Popular contemporary evangelical views of ancient Christian teaching frequently hold that the classic writers almost wholly ignored the doctrine of justification. Where it is discussed, the fantasy is that they denied the imputation of the righteousness of God in Christ to sinners. They allegedly confused justification with personal virtue, and they did not pay much attention to Paul's key passages on justification. But I must textually prove that allegation.

The esteemed Reformed teacher, Louis Berkhof, is typical: "The doctrine of justification by faith was not always clearly understood. In fact, it did not find its classical expression until the days of the Reformation. . . . Some of the earliest Church Fathers already speak of justification by faith, but it is quite evident that they had no clear understanding of it and of its relation to faith."[1] Berkhof argued that Clement of Alexandria, Origen, Irenaeus, and Tertullian all failed to understand the doctrine of justification. He regards them as moralists out of sync with Paul. Allegedly they were not clear about the justifying action of God upon which faith is based. Faith often seems to them to be an intellectual assent, or even complete self-surrender to Christ, but it appeared to lack the sense of a saving trust in the finished work of Christ.

Similarly, we hear this judgment from a leading contemporary theological work: "The early fathers of the church, occupied with pressing Christological and Trinitarian controversies, did not explore in depth the doctrine of justification by faith. The first serious study of justification was undertaken by Augustine in the fourth century. Not until the personal discovery that Martin Luther made was the forensic interpretation of justification developed in detail."[2] These assumptions are still widely believed by

---

1. *Systematic Theology* (Grand Rapids: Eerdmans, 1938), p. 511.
2. Gordon R. Lewis and Bruce A. Demarest, *Integrative Theology* (Grand Rapids: Zondervan, 1996), 3:133-34.

many sincere evangelicals, despite compelling contrary evidence, which we will set forth.

Although Augustine is of all the ancient Christian writers the one who stands closest to Protestant teachings of salvation by grace alone, and the teacher who most powerfully influenced the Reformation writers, even he ironically becomes portrayed by some evangelicals as a culprit. "There is [in Augustine] a deplorable absence of an emphatic distinction between justification and sanctification as Paul and Luther had it."[3] The assumption is that Luther finally got right what Augustine got wrong.[4]

It is widely imagined by evangelical historians that "Augustine's system parted company with Paulinism, and opened the way to the re-establishment of salvation by merit." "Grace was represented as a supernatural life infused into human nature through sacramental channels and gradually built up into a righteousness which was not meritorious only because it was imparted rather than achieved." It is commonly argued that "Augustine clearly subsumed under justification what Protestants understand by regeneration and sanctification."[5] "When describing salvation Augustine preferred these terms [predestination, calling, glorification, regeneratio, vivificatio, renovatio, and sanctificatio] to justification. Later Roman Catholic theology expanded on the Augustinian notion that justification is the process that actually makes a person righteous."[6]

According to Lutheran theologian Bengt Haegglund, the apostolic fathers, excepting Clement of Rome, had little in common with Paul's emphasis on justification by faith. He claims that it is not unmerited grace that stands at the center of patristic teaching but rather, the new way of life that Christ taught and which he empowers.[7] Only belatedly in the sixteenth century, he argues, was there a reliable discovery of the New Testament doctrine of justification.[8]

---

3. J. L. Neve, *History of Christian Thought* (Philadelphia: Muhlenberg, 1946), 1:146.

4. Alister McGrath argues that Augustine did not understand justification as did the Reformers, and lent a hand to its misinterpretation (*Iustitia Dei* [Cambridge: Cambridge University Press, 1986], 1:60).

5. Lewis and Demarest, *Integrative Theology*, 3:127-28.

6. Lewis and Demarest, *Integrative Theology*, 3:127-28.

7. Haegglund, *History of Theology* (Saint Louis: Concordia, 1966), p. 17.

8. See also J. G. J. Simpson on Justification in J. Hastings, *Encyclopedia of Religion and Ethics* (Edinburgh: T. and T. Clark, 1908-26), 7:618.

This Reader seeks to correct these common assumptions, and to do this by an overwhelming presentation of evidence to the contrary.

6. Liberal Misconceptions

Not only evangelical but also liberal writers have missed the richness of classical Christian exegetes on salvation by grace through faith. What follows are evidences, easily duplicated, that show how liberal theology over its opulent century of opportunity did not bother to study carefully ancient Christian salvation teaching.

The liberals were far more interested in imposing their own modern ideological bent upon these texts than allowing them to speak for themselves. The liberal historians and exegetes basically agreed: if you want to understand faith, do not go to Chrysostom or Augustine, go to Jesus and Paul, or better, selected passages of Jesus and Paul, filtered through a nineteenth-century ideological sieve. Liberal theology commonly denies that the blood Christ shed on the cross was a payment for sins or a legal imputation of the alien righteousness of Christ to sinners.[9]

Liberals often construed justification in the end as ethical improvement effected voluntarily and humanistically by free moral agents — the very opposite of classical ecumenical teaching. The liberals sometimes used patristic sources selectively to support their views, but more commonly rejected patristic sources because they perceived them as outmoded and biased. These sources were seldom considered in their wholeness and complexity as serious exegetical arguments.

Liberals have been typically offended by the view that the holy God judges sin. They prefer to talk exclusively of the love of God rather than placing the love of God in the context of God's holiness and just judgment of sin. Liberal theologies often argued that there is no anger or wrath in God, and assumed that there is no serious sin to be sacrificially propitiated, forgiven, and corrected. They imagined that love can be considered as if apart from divine judgment, holiness, and justice.

---

9. Cf. Albrecht Ritschl, *The Christian Doctrine of Justification and Reconciliation* (Clifton, N.J.: Reference Book Publishers, 1966), p. 274, followed by a long train of onion-peeling writers from Adolf von Harnack through Albert Schweitzer to Edgar Sheffield Brightman and John Spong.

Liberal theologies of justification, whether liberal Protestant or liberal Catholic, were enamored of a universalistic tendency that goes counter to the classic teaching of recalcitrant sin. Prevenient grace saves every time: "Every human person, by reason of birth and of God's universal offer of grace, is already called to be a child of God and an heir of heaven."[10] They saw justification as the human emulation of the supposed moral ideals of Jesus by which they attain by example a higher level of moral development that allows them to reconcile themselves to God.[11] In these responses they were reacting less to ancient consensual teaching than to medieval Catholic scholasticism and corrupt church abuses and the late sixteenth-century dogmas of Trent. In this reaction, Protestant liberals and conservatives alike continue sadly to regard the first five centuries of scriptural interpretation through the dated and jaded eyes of sixteenth-century polemics.

Since Ritschl and Harnack, it has been widely and erroneously accepted by both liberal and conservative teachers that among the church fathers "there is an imperceptible yet growing departure from the fundamental doctrine of salvation, as it had been set forth by Paul," accompanied by "an adoption of a more legal view, in which faith is identified with doctrinal belief, and hence is coupled with works, instead of being their fruitful source."[12] Fisher argued that in the apostolic fathers "the Pauline doctrine of justification [is] seldom brought out" in a "clear and positive form." One finds instead "an importance laid upon right conduct, and upon works of obedience, which is somewhat in contrast with the manner of St. Paul when he is defining the method of justification."[13] Liberal Christians often argued that the early Christians were "simply reproducing Paul's idea without appreciating what it involved."[14]

Later liberals reduced justification to deliverance of the oppressed from social and political bondage.[15] Process theology tended to reject Paul's teaching of forensic imputation of Christ's righteousness, substitut-

---

10. Richard P. McBrien, *Catholicism* (Minneapolis: Winston, 1981), p. 423.

11. Shailer Matthews, *The Faith of Modernism* (New York: Macmillan, 1924), p. 183.

12. G. P. Fisher, *The Reformation* (New York: Scribner, 1884), p. 16.

13. Fisher, *History of Christian Thought,* 2nd edition (Edinburgh: T. & T. Clark, 1896), p. 42.

14. A. C. McGiffert, *A History of Christian Thought* (New York: Scribner, 1932), p. 85.

15. James Cone, *God of the Oppressed* (New York: Seabury, 1975), p. 229.

ing for it the idea of the divine approval of positive human responses to the divine lure, optimally displayed in Jesus.[16]

Albert Schweitzer is typical among German liberals in his belief that the apostolic fathers did not grasp the heart of Pauline teaching. The early Fathers "know him, but they owe no allegiance to him. . . . The theology of an Ignatius or a Justin does not attach itself to him. There is something more in this than a simple oversight here."[17] Schweitzer thought that the inability of the post-apostolic writers to claim and own the teaching of Paul was due to the decline in the urgency of the end-time expectation. The delay of the return of the Lord had supposedly encouraged a Christ-mysticism that misplaced Pauline justification teaching as a doctrine closely related to the expected judgment of the end time. So the end result has been a neglect of patristic exegesis by both liberal and evangelical Protestantism.

B. The Unexplored Connection: The Fathers
Were Not Ignorant of the Pauline Teaching of Justification

1. What Is Meant by "Patristic"?

When I use the terms "patristic" and "classic exegetes" and "Fathers," I am referring to pre-Protestant, pre-European, pre-medieval exegetes of the first half of the first millennium.

Who are these principal sources of classic Christian exegesis? Especially those who early gained the most general consent throughout the Asian, African, and western church traditions as universally esteemed: eight great doctors of the church — especially Athanasius, Basil, Gregory Nazianzus, and John Chrysostom in the East, and Ambrose, Jerome, Augustine, and Gregory the Great in the West.

Among these, Chrysostom and Augustine were most emphatic and influential regarding questions of saving faith. In addition to these eight,

16. Norman Pittenger, *Cosmic Love and Human Wrong* (New York: Paulist, 1978), and *Freed to Love: A Process Interpretation of Redemption* (Wilton, Conn.: Morehouse-Barlow, 1987), pp. 68-71.

17. Albert Schweitzer, *Paul and His Interpreters*, trans. W. Montgomery (New York: Schocken Books, 1964), p. 248, from *Geschichte der Paulinischen Forschung*, 1911.

there are a number of widely respected classic Christian teachers cited by various ecumenical councils as most generally reliable to the church in all its eastern and western and African varieties: Cyprian of Carthage, Cyril of Jerusalem, Gregory of Nyssa, Ambrosiaster, Cyril of Alexandria, Leo I, and John of Damascus. All of these were specifically acknowledged by general ancient councils as reliable and consensual.

By "consensual" I do not imply that there was no variety of interpretation under the vast umbrella of orthodox consent. Rather the opposite: the varieties were embraced and transmuted. A worldwide consenting community freely received these exegetes as standing faithfully within the East and West consensus defined by the early ecumenical councils (excepting those rare instances where even these exegetes failed to gain general consent).

2. The Unity of the First Five Centuries Contrasted with the Conflict of the Last Five Centuries

The evidence will show that there is a stable, explicit, consensual tradition of exegesis of Paul's teaching of justification *by grace alone through faith alone*. It was firmly established long before Luther or John Calvin or the rending debates of Augsburg and Trent in the sixteenth century, which were chiefly about medieval scholastic distortions of patristic teaching.

The Reformers rightly combated these distortions. I will show that key texts on justification, especially Ephesians 2 and Romans 3, were thoroughly and critically examined by the ancient Christian writers and understood in much the same way that they were to be later rediscovered by the Reformation writers in their struggle against the medieval distortions. I am not arguing that there were no ambiguities in patristic teaching on justification — one can always find non-consensual aberrations and debates — but that there *is* strong central affirmation of the Pauline doctrine of justification in the patristic writers, which later became the defining doctrine of the Reformation.

Among patristic exegetes there were admittedly many differences of cultural assumptions, literary style, idiomatic language, and symbol systems, just as there were among the Reformers. But there is a remarkable level of general consensus precisely on justification by grace through faith, the very doctrine that has so sundered the church of the last five centuries.

My thesis is so simple and clear that I am amazed there is so little recognition of it in the literature: *I am contrasting the unity of the first five centuries on justification teaching with the disunity of the last five centuries on justification teaching.*

The good news: Most of what patristic writers teach on justification by grace through faith can be confessed in good conscience by contemporary Christians who speak out of many different church memories, out of dissimilar histories and liturgical practices: Russian Orthodox, South American Pentecostal, Chinese Roman Catholic, Ugandan Anglican. The bad news is that both Protestants and Catholics still have deep-seated polemical resistance even to examining this shared textual history.

In exploring this thesis, I invite Protestant colleagues to admonish me fairly and precisely about what is substantively missing in these patristic justification passages that would be required to pass muster by rigorous classic Protestant teaching standards. I propose that this patristic teaching is profoundly in accord with strict Lutheran and Reformed teaching on justification, from Melanchthon and Bucer to Gerhard and Owen to Hodge. But that is just the hypothesis that we must fairly and openly debate.

Among my most respected contemporary colleagues are Alister McGrath, R. C. Sproul, and Michael Horton. All of them would agree, I believe, that there are patristic intimations of the Protestant teaching of justification. But I am less sure that they would agree with me concerning the extent and depth of that teaching as being already deeply embedded in ancient Christian exegesis of Paul. Although I do not think of my primary audience as these highly articulate scholars, but rather the laity, I would welcome their thoughtful examination of this argument.

The only way to establish and confirm this thesis is to present the evidence. I choose to do so largely without the intrusion of my own personalized commentary. I want to allow the texts to speak for themselves. In the interest of permitting patristic writers their own voice, it is time to resist the temptation to make extensive "reader response" speculations on the ways that contemporary Christians tend to read patristic texts with entirely different subjective memories, nuances, and dispositions. Rather, let the patristic texts themselves form the basis for a potentially promising evangelical-ecumenical dialogue on the unity of the body of Christ.

A gradually increasing expression of the unity of the body of Christ is being discovered among Orthodox, Protestants, and Catholics, but sadly this often occurs without the power of the textual evidence of the consensual teachers of the paleo-ecumenical doctrine of justification. So the textual evidence must now be directly set forth without intrusion in order that fewer biases accompany their presentation. I have deliberately preferred texts with rhetorically strong content, texts that display the power to convince without the need of extensive contextualization.

3. Remembering the Fathers' Continuous Immersion in the Written Word

Sola scriptura is generally regarded as a distinctive Protestant theme. But remember that the pattern of assuming that the scriptures are the judge of the church is a fixed guideline in patristic teaching.

Those who doubt the depth of scriptural immersion among the early homilists would do well to read their commentaries on scripture to correct that illusion, especially their ability to compare scripture with scripture. Many early Christian teachers memorized vast passages of the New Testament, and many more memorized all the Psalms. More scripture was steadily read in the round of Orthodox and Catholic daily and weekly scripture readings during a given year than is typically read by many modern Protestants. The stereotype of the pre-Protestant tradition as keeping scripture under lock and key is largely a picture shaped by polemics against late medieval scholasticism. It is not a picture of the church in its first five centuries.

4. The Practical Impact

The practical impact and outcome of this evidence is that Orthodox, Catholics, and Protestants can, insofar as they are willing to set aside unfounded stereotypes and prejudices, find joyful and unexpected common ground in the first millennium of scripture interpretation for the very doctrine that most divided them after the sixteenth century.

I have been privileged to serve on a half dozen major international consultations between evangelicals and Orthodox, and between evangelicals and Catholics. These include evangelical-Orthodox conversations in

Stuttgart in 1994 and in Alexandria in 1996, and ongoing World Evangelical Alliance–Roman Catholic conversations in Jerusalem, Chicago, Lake Geneva, and Swanick, England. In these conversations I have often been asked to show evidence of my claim that classic texts on justification teaching predate the watershed events of the sixteenth century.

What follows is this evidence. It shows that Orthodox, Catholics, classic Protestants, charismatics, and the heirs of pietistic revivalism today all have a right to appeal to the same faithful ancient consensual church teachers and scriptural interpreters. The divided church does not have to remain forever fixated on the sixteenth-century polemics that have so sundered Christianity. The Holy Spirit is leading the body of Christ now toward greater ownership of first-millennium texts to reach for a post-liberal orthodox consensus.

The classic consensus-bearing interpreters of Paul's letters give contemporary Protestants (whether Baptists, Calvinists, Wesleyans, Lutherans, holiness tradition faithful, or Pentecostals) a fresh opportunity to focus anew on the underlying thread of consensuality to which all Christians can confidently point as a solidly shared textual tradition, preserved by the grace of the Holy Spirit through centuries of changing times. The same faith was taught by those with such varied cultures as Isaac of Nineveh, Cyprian of Carthage, and Irenaeus of Lyon, and by such diverse Protestant writers as Melanchthon, John Owen, Wesley, and Spurgeon.

Some Protestants may imagine that contemporary Greek Orthodox and Roman Catholic writers are still thoroughly engrossed in patristic teaching. Regrettably this can no longer be counted upon. It is too often only a thin veneer under which there is a prevailing accommodation to modern thought patterns. The fixation of Roman Catholics upon modern Vatican II teaching has led to the neglect of ancient ecumenical teaching, despite Vatican II appeals to the contrary. The defensiveness of many Orthodox teachers against both Protestantism and Roman Catholicism has led to a defensive myopia that fails to recognize the implications of the deep classic consensus that is represented in the texts we will examine.

Orthodox are not noted for reading western patristic texts. Catholics neglect eastern sources. Protestants doubly neglect both. The texts ahead will show the profound possibility of all these grounding themselves together in classic Christian teaching, which can become a means of rediscovering the already present level of unity of the body of Christ worldwide. The lack of access to these sources has stood as a formidable block to the unity of the body of Christ.

5. Why Dangerous? The Alarming Consequence
of the Rediscovery of the Unity of the Body of Christ

This is a dangerous argument because if understood and accepted, it could end in dismantling the polemics industry that feeds off distrust between Protestants and Catholics, and between Orthodox and all supposed latecomers.

This polemics industry undoubtedly exists. It has money, presses, air time, attractive spokespersons, and an anxiety-prone following. It raises its money from fear of an imaginary opponent, the disbeliever who has the same scripture but with a deficient liturgical or ecclesiological memory — the supposed enemy who was baptized by someone else. But these opponents are often mirror images of anxious modern imaginations. The imagination feeds on exaggeration of the supposed disbelief of the "other." I intend to show that these "others" are much more akin to ourselves than we would wish to believe. We will let the texts teach us of this decisive but unrecognized consensus. They reground orthodox Protestants, orthodox Catholics, and evangelical Orthodox.

In places like Cuba and China these polemics have tragically weakened Christian witness. The politicians of Cuba and China would much prefer to see Christians fighting each other than celebrating their unity in the body of Christ.

Bigoted and tendentious assumptions are found equally among Catholics, Orthodox, charismatics, evangelicals, and liberals, not only in Cuba and China but in Chicago and Sao Paulo. I will present texts of key consensual witnesses of Christian writers of the earliest Christian centuries to show clearly that they had a firm grasp of justification teaching: *sola gratia*, *sola fide*, and *sola scriptura* (grace alone, faith alone, scripture alone).

6. Why Does This Recognition Have a Painful Edge for Protestants?

Why is it so difficult, so painful, for Protestants to give up the illusion that no other Christians had ever discovered justification before Luther? Pride plays into this. The fantasy is a part of the core infrastructure of popular Protestant identity and polemics. It is the heart of the Protestant defensive armory. It helps to provide a rationale for why Protestant doctrine exists, as a biblical corrective to virtually all previous Christian experience. Protestants tend to idealize their history of rescuing Paul from medieval scholasticism. It was indeed good and salutary that Protestantism effected this rescue. But it is painful now to realize that this was not a rescue from all pre-Protestant interpreters, but rather a rescue from only ancillary distortions of patristic thought that developed in the late middle ages.

If this Reader is persuasive, it will be harder for Catholics to ignore Protestant teaching on salvation that is grounded in their own most valued historic sources, and for Protestants to dismiss the earliest tap roots of pre-Reformation classic Catholic teaching. When it becomes textually clear that the doctrines thought to be uniquely discovered by Protestantism were already embedded in the mainstream teaching of the ancient ecumenical writers, the relation has fundamentally changed.

7. Can Christian Teaching Be Trusted If It Lacks Scriptural Grounding and an Orthodox Historical Textuary?

This Reader provides an example of how to mesh exegetical theology, historical theology, systematic theology, and ecumenical theology. It shows how anyone can think systematically about a particular locus of theology in an orthodox manner by reference to key scripture texts that authenticate that theological point, and by examining what the history of interpretation says about those texts, and whether they can be shown to exhibit a plausible ecumenical consensus in all Christian centuries.

Ph.D. dissertations are now being written with this method in view. The subject matter is history of exegesis. Is this a historical study? Is it a biblical study? Is it an exercise in systematic theology? Is it an ecumenical exercise? Yes, on all counts.

It is doubtful that a theology that lacks any of these characteristics can be trusted by the laity. The faithful look toward the clergy to pass on to them the true gospel, not some private speculation. This way of working theologically seeks to correct the subjectivism, reductionism, and faddism so long rife in modern theology.

8. Ecumenical Dialogue Needs These Arguments

Two recent documents are significant in moving toward establishing contemporary consensual views of justification: "The Gospel of Jesus Christ

— An Evangelical Celebration" states the evangelical consensus. In the "Joint Declaration on the Doctrine of Justification" (hereafter JD), the Lutheran World Federation and the Roman Catholic Church attempt to state their current level of official consensus. I wish to show that both of these recent statements are substantially consistent with the consensus established in the patristic period, but in need of much further evidentiary study.

As a drafter of the Roman Catholic–World Evangelical Alliance documents, and of the Evangelicals and Catholics Together document on "The Gift of Salvation," I have been grateful for all these efforts. But what is now needed is more patristic input.

The Catholic-Lutheran Joint Declaration, by the absence of substantive patristic references, poses the problem to which this Justification Reader exists as a response. A close reading of the Joint Declaration makes it evident that virtually all its normative Catholic references come out of modern Catholic sources. While there are many key patristic assumptions in these sources, few are directly quoted in the Joint Declaration. Rather, the strong focus on Tridentine arguments seems to imply a supposed lacuna of patristic sources. There are frequent quotations of Luther, the Formula of Concord, Trent, Vatican II, the Pontifical Council, and modern ecumenical documents, but without ancient ecumenical reference.

My premise in the Justification Reader, as it will be in all the Reader Series, is that ancient Christian writers offer reliable scriptural analyses that bring Orthodox, Catholics, and Protestants closer together in joint ownership of a common ancient ecumenical theological tradition. This is far harder to argue with medieval, Reformation, and post-Reformation than with patristic documents.

A few of my conservative evangelical friends (from both Reformed and revivalist traditions) have treated the Joint Declaration as a sellout to equivocation. Most of these critics, however, still want to locate their arguments in Reformation, not patristic, sources. The way ahead for future reconciliation is through the earliest ecumenical consensus. The energy of the polemical Tridentine debates is exhausted. I am trying to transcend this exhaustion by appealing to texts that are jointly owned by the whole Christian tradition.

When I have spoken with widely different theologians like Avery Dulles, Michael Horton, Timothy George, William Rusch, Richard Neuhaus, and Wolfhart Pannenberg about the striking absence of patristic testimony in the justification debate to date, they have strongly encouraged me to show the evidence. They say they have not seen it fully and clearly laid out. That is what the Justification Reader is for. Thus far no one has yet presented these patristic arguments as grist for the ecumenical mill.

It would be possible to extend this book by many hundreds of pages by adding a substantial section that would unpack the Reformation, Counter-Reformation, and modern arguments on justification. But this is not my vocation, since so many have already attempted that, and so few (including the Pontifical Council for Promoting Christian Unity and the Lutheran World Federation) have seriously addressed the patristic texts on justification.

9. Assessing the Joint Declaration

In the sixteenth century the Reformation and Counter-Reformation doctrinal condemnations of each other on justification were set over against each other in highly polemical and defensive language. The Lutheran-Catholic Joint Declaration rightly argues that this doctrine "came into particular prominence in the Reformation period," but it fails to establish that the pre-Reformation texts on justification were clearly articulated and fully understood before the Reformation. This is our present task. The Joint Declaration, like this study, seeks to articulate a common understanding of Christians on justification. But it does so primarily "by appropriating insights of recent biblical studies" (JD 2.13), whereas it might more fruitfully have inquired further into patristic sources for this common understanding.

Among the conclusions of the Joint Declaration with which the Fathers generally agree are that justifying faith "includes hope in God and love for him. Such a faith is active in love, and thus the Christian cannot and should not remain without works. But whatever in the justified precedes or follows the free gift of faith is neither the basis of justification nor merits it" (JD 4.3.25). "Justification remains free from human cooperation and is not dependent on the life-regenerating effects of grace in human beings" (JD 4.2.23). "God no longer imputes to them [believers] their sin and through the Holy Spirit effects in them an active love" (JD 4.2). They agree that "By justification we are both declared and made righteous. Justification, therefore, is not a legal fiction. God, in justifying, effects what he promises; he forgives sin and makes us truly righteous" (JD p. 31). Such conclusions are consensually anticipated by the ancient Christian writers.

The Joint Declaration states a Lutheran-Catholic "consensus on basic truths of the doctrine of justification and shows that the remaining differences in its explication are no longer the occasion for doctrinal condemnations" (JD Preamble 4). By this declaration "the subscribing Lutheran churches and the Roman Catholic Church are now able to articulate a common understanding of our justification by God's grace through faith in Christ" (JD Preamble 5). The Joint Declaration is confident that Catholics and Lutherans now can express together "a shared understanding of justification. This encompasses a consensus in the basic truths; the differing explications in particular statements are compatible with it" (JD 3.14). The Joint Declaration concludes that "The teaching of the Lutheran churches presented in this Declaration does not fall under the condemnations of the Council of Trent. The condemnations of the Lutheran Confessions do not apply to the teaching of the Roman Catholic Church presented in this Declaration" (JD 5.41). Yet without ancient ecumenical consensual texts, the Joint Declaration has not shed the appearance of being more a political than an exegetical achievement.

10. The Growing Hunger for Greater Evangelical Unity in the Gospel

I will take as a consensual statement of contemporary Protestant teaching on justification the statement on "The Gospel of Jesus Christ" (hereafter GJC), which has emerged out of the Billy Graham Organization, *Christianity Today,* and an impressive list of varied evangelical signers. This confession intends to provide a unified consensual statement of gospel teaching for evangelicals the world over.

This most powerful document representing evangelical consensus in our time is worth quoting here explicitly: "We know that divisions among Christians hinder our witness in the world, and we desire greater mutual understanding and truth-speaking in love. We know too that as trustees of God's revealed truth we cannot embrace any form of doctrinal indifferentism, or relativism, or pluralism by which God's truth is sacrificed for a false peace" (GJC). "Doctrinal disagreements call for debate. Dialogue for mutual understanding and, if possible, narrowing of the differences is

32

valuable, doubly so when the avowed goal is unity in primary things, with liberty in secondary things, and charity in all things" (GJC).

"The Bible declares that all who truly trust in Christ and his Gospel are sons and daughters of God through grace, and hence are our brothers and sisters in Christ. All who are justified experience reconciliation with the Father, full remission of sins, transition from the kingdom of darkness to the kingdom of light, the reality of being a new creature in Christ, and the fellowship of the Holy Spirit. They enjoy access to the Father with all the peace and joy that this brings" (GJC).

"This Gospel is the only Gospel: there is no other; and to change its substance is to pervert and indeed destroy it. This Gospel is so simple that small children can understand it, and it is so profound that studies by the wisest theologians will never exhaust its riches. All Christians are called to unity in love and unity in truth. As evangelicals who derive our very name from the Gospel, we celebrate this great good news of God's saving work in Jesus Christ as the true bond of Christian unity, whether among organized churches and denominations or in the many transdenominational cooperative enterprises of Christians together" (GJC).

In this Celebration "an attempt has been made to state what is primary and essential in the Gospel as evangelicals understand it. Useful dialogue, however, requires not only charity in our attitudes, but also clarity in our utterances. Our extended analysis of justification by faith alone through Christ alone reflects our belief that Gospel truth is of crucial importance and is not always well understood and correctly affirmed. For added clarity, out of love for God's truth and Christ's church, we now cast the key points of what has been said into specific affirmations and denials regarding the Gospel and our unity in it and in Christ" (GJC).

Nothing in this Celebration runs counter to the patristic exegesis developed in what follows.

11. *The Search for Balance and the Hazard*
    of Presenting Too Little Evidence or Too Much

I have tried to strike a balance between offering too much or too little evidence in demonstrating the unity of Christian teaching on justifying grace by faith alone. I can understand that some would wish more and some less. To those who warn that this book is too heavy for the impatient lay reader,

I answer: I can only pray that providential grace will lead me to a vital meeting with my intended audience.

I am reaching out for laity who already understand the undisputed and sweeping importance of this topic — their own salvation! They do not have to be convinced that it requires a serious immersion in the Word of God. This book is not for the casual passerby who wants a fast food order. It seeks no "best seller" status in book marketing. It seeks out the maturing lay believer who loves the Word, delights in meditating on it, and cannot get enough of bathing in the mystery of the Gospel. If occasional repetition occurs, despite much culling, it offers another opportunity to savor the mystery of grace.

These documents are available only in highly scattered sources, often in antiquated sources, or in creedal collections or in musty source books of patrology or historical theology, and available there only in limited ways. It would require of a reader a great deal of ingenuity and effort to bring all these sources together in single argument. Some of them will be found in the *Ancient Christian Commentary on Scripture*, but there are many here that do not appear there, and all of those volumes will be some years in appearing. I do indeed enjoy the advantage of having much of that textual material before me as its General Editor. But it would take the novice reader thousands of hours to find these texts and put them in a harmonious argument. Meanwhile the dialogue on evangelical unity will not wait.

Even if you had these dispersed sources all between the covers of one book, it would take a great deal of effort to see how they were correlated in a cohesive argument. You do not have to make the search, because it has now been made and the results set forth in an orderly argument. Critics may wish to question my criteria for selection, or my ordering of the selections, but they can no longer question that these texts exist, and that they are substantially congruent. It is the very existence of justification texts prior to the Reformation that I wish to demonstrate.

It is just because such a book does not exist, and to my knowledge has never existed, that I have felt called upon to gather this source material in a Reader format and write a cohesive unified argument that draws into a unity these widely different texts.

I have attempted to discuss justification in previous studies, but neither within this compass nor with a view toward comparing patristic and Reformation teaching. For those who might wish to see these earlier attempts at more technical or more limited forays into this subject, please refer to *The Transforming Power of Grace* and *Life in the Spirit* (pp. 108-77), where I have attempted to define a classic consensual teaching of justification, grace, faith, and good works, focusing especially on the earliest Christian consensual sources. Some ideas discussed in those studies have been either adapted or amended or tempered in these pages to accommodate to the style and purposes of this Reader. Here they are clarified in simpler modern English, and backed up textually.

12. Fairly Assessing the Evidence

To make a case in evidentiary presentation requires actually presenting the evidence. Think of me as an attorney defending my clients — in this case the key exponents of classic Christian justification teaching. My clients' reputations have been damaged unjustly. My clients (the ancient Christian writers) have been charged with not remembering rightly — for fifteen centuries, right up until Luther! Any suggestion that Christian teaching has rightly understood justification before Luther meets with cynical guffaws in some circles. The prosecutor, according to this awkward analogy, is modern Protestantism, which still cherishes the fantasy that no one ever understood justification before Luther, except possibly Paul and maybe not even him.

If I made a haphazard summary presentation of evidence, my clients would not be well served. No. I must plan the presentation of evidence carefully, so that the conclusion of the jury — you — will be obvious, inescapable, and undeniable. If I present my clients' case too hastily, the prosecutor will certainly say: "He hasn't decisively proved his point that there is indeed an ancient Christian consensus on justification teaching." I have tried to reach a balance, but I suspect that more of my academic critics will think I have written too little; more of my lay readers will think I have written too much. So be it.

In taking up the question of justification, we are asking exclusively about what God has done to acquit sin. Only after dealing with the new relation with the Judge are we in a position to think about our fitting moral responses to grace. Only when our lives are hid in Christ are we ready to understand how we are to answer behaviorally and responsibly to this merciful Judge.

CHAPTER TWO

Justification Defined

How is justification defined in classic Christian teaching — based on scripture, ancient ecumenical consensus, and the Protestant Confessions?

A. Rehearsing the Classic Consensus on Justification

1. What Is Justification?

What is Justification? Justification is the declaration of God that one who trusts in Christ's atoning work, however sinful, is treated or accounted as righteous. This credited righteousness is received by faith.

This is not to be viewed as if it were merely a legal fiction, or as a fantasy imagined in God's mind, or as a human hypothetical conjecture. This uprighted relation with the holy God comes about as a decisive, merciful divine act, an actual event in history that occurs on the cross.

Justification is the reversal of God's judgment against the sinner, in which the sinner is declared to be no longer exposed to the penalty of the law, which is ultimately spiritual death, but restored to divine favor. Justification is that divine act by which one stands now in a right relation with God. It is an act of God's free grace through which the sinner is absolved from guilt and accepted as righteous on account of the Son's atoning work.

Justification is the pardoning act of the supreme Judge of all, by which he pardons *all* the sins of those who trust in the pardoning work of

Christ in our place on the cross. In this way the righteousness of Christ is applied to the believer.

It is not that the law is blandly relaxed or dishonestly set aside. Rather, the law is declared to be fulfilled in an even stricter sense: by the Judge himself, by his own sacrificial offering of himself as he himself fulfills the requirements of the law for us! This happens by imputing or crediting to the believer by God himself the perfect righteousness of his representative and guarantee: God the Son, Jesus Christ (Rom. 10:3-9). Justification is not the forgiveness of a man without righteousness, but a declaration that he possesses a righteousness that perfectly and forever satisfies the law, namely Christ's righteousness (2 Cor. 5:21; Rom. 4:6-8). The sole condition on which this righteousness is imputed or credited to the believer is faith in the Lord Jesus Christ, who is at the same time truly man and truly God.

Justification is the opposite of condemnation. One is justified who is viewed as right with the Judge, the law, and the Lawgiver (Apology of the Augsburg Confession, IV.[1] The justifying Judge declares that all the requirements of the law are entirely satisfied. The person justified is declared to be entitled to all the advantages and rewards arising from perfect obedience to the law (Rom. 5:1-10).

Hence this simple formula is often heard in Protestant teaching on justification:

- Its Source: God.
- Its Nature: a gracious act.
- Its Elements: pardon and acceptance.
- Its Scope: all believers.
- Its Ground: the imputed righteousness of Christ.
- Its Condition: faith alone.

Justification does not result from higher commitment to greater ideals or more advanced actualization of good character or better performance of the demands of the law. It is solely due to a declaration of God's merciful attitude toward the sinner whose life is hid in Christ.

---

1. BOC, pp. 107ff.

2. The Way to Consensus

Having defined our subject, we now make a transition. In the preceding we have been led by scripture to define the core of the doctrine of justification by grace through faith. But does this definition hold for all Christian traditions, all centuries, Catholic, Orthodox, and Protestant?

We must first establish whether this teaching is indeed shared by the most reliable and authoritative and defining sources of Protestant teaching. Then we will speak of the ancient ecumenical orthodox consensual teaching.

Is there an underlying Protestant consensus on justification? And is it preceded by a patristic consensus? Our core argument: There is a classical Christian consensual teaching of justification that embraces both the patristic teachers and the orthodox Protestant teachers.

All classic Protestant confessions stand strictly under the authority of scripture. Their major purpose is to bring scriptural teaching into a concise statement for preaching and teaching purposes.

Although it would be an easy matter to set forth in a multi-column graph the comparative language of Protestant confessions on justification, the exercise would be superfluous and repetitive. Why? Because the language of these confessions typically repeats almost verbatim the language of scripture. For interested readers, especially of the Reformed traditions, this has already been done by a number of readily available collections: See *A Harmony of Westminster Presbyterian Standards with Explanatory Notes;*[2] *The Creeds of Christendom,* vol. 3;[3] Thomas C. Oden, *Doctrinal Standards in the Wesleyan Tradition;*[4] and *Documents of the English Reformation.*[5] Although they are not presented in graph-comparative form, the reader can easily consult *Creeds of the Churches*[6] and *Confessions and Catechisms of the Reformation*[7] to confirm the consensuality of this justification teaching.

I will select a few of these texts on justifying grace in order that the reader can observe and be reassured that this consensual teaching is strongly confirmed by authoritative Protestant texts. This consensual teaching does not exist as a project of imagination. It exists textually, historically, objectively.

2. Ed. James Benjamin Green (Richmond, Va.: John Knox Press, 1951).
3. Ed. P. Schaff (Grand Rapids: Baker, 1931 ed. reprinted 1985).
4. (Grand Rapids: Zondervan, 1988).
5. Ed. Gerald Bray (Minneapolis: Fortress Press, 1994).
6. Ed. John H. Leith (Atlanta: John Knox Press, 3rd ed. 1982).
7. Ed. Mark A. Noll (Grand Rapids: Baker, 1991).

3. Representative Reformed Confessions on Justification

The French Reformed Confession of Faith, 1559, Article XVIII states: "We therefore reject all other means of justification before God, and without claiming any virtue or merit, we rest simply in the obedience of Jesus Christ, which is imputed to us as much to blot out all our sins as to make us find grace and favor in the sight of God."[8]

The Belgic Confession, 1561, article XXII: "We do not mean that faith itself justifies us, for it is only an instrument with which we embrace Christ our Righteousness."[9]

The most widely received and authoritative Reformed confession is the Westminster Confession (1646), whose eleventh article, Of Justification, reads: "Those whom God effectually calls, He also freely justifies; not by infusing righteousness into them, but by pardoning their sins, and by accounting and accepting their persons as righteous; not for anything wrought in them, or done by them, but for Christ's sake alone; nor by imputing faith itself, the act of believing, or any other evangelical obedience to them, as their righteousness; but by imputing the obedience and satisfaction of Christ unto them, they receiving and resting on Him and His righteousness by faith; which faith they have not of themselves, it is the gift of God." That says it all.

Similarly the accompanying Westminster Larger Catechism asks the person whose baptism is being confirmed: "Q. 70. What is justification? A. Justification is an act of God's free grace unto sinners, in which he pardons all their sin, accepts and accounts their persons righteous in his sight, not for anything wrought in them, or done by them, but only for the perfect obedience and full satisfaction of Christ, by God imputed to them, and received by faith alone." If this is beginning to seem repetitive, that is the very point I seek to establish.

The Westminster Shorter Catechism is for the instruction of children who come to the Lord's table: "Question 33: What is justification? Answer 33: Justification is an act of God's free grace, wherein he pardons all our sins, and accepts us as righteous in his sight, only for the righteousness of Christ imputed to us, and received by faith alone." Same teaching, slightly different words.

8. COC 3:370.
9. COC 3:408.

These authoritative confessions are sufficient enough that, without further repetition, we can conclude that the Reformed doctrinal tradition strongly upholds the Pauline doctrine of justification. These same teachings are confirmed in Lutheran, Baptist, Anglican, and Wesleyan traditions, a selection of which follows.

4. The Lutheran Formula of Concord

An Epitome of the Articles found in the Lutheran Formula of Concord, 1576, which sets the pattern for much subsequent consensual Protestant teaching on justification, reads: "Article III. Preface, Of the Righteousness of Faith Before God: It is taught in our churches that we most wretched sinners are justified before God and saved alone by faith in Christ, so that Christ alone is our righteousness. Now this Jesus Christ, our Savior and our righteousness, is true God and true man."[10]

5. Baptist Confessions

The New Hampshire Baptist Confession, 1833, Article V, Of Justification, states: "We believe that the great gospel blessing which Christ secures to such as believe in him is Justification; that Justification includes the pardon of sin, and the promise of eternal life on principles of righteousness; that it is bestowed, not in consideration of any works of righteousness which we have done, but solely through faith in the Redeemer's blood."[11]

Young persons in the English Baptist tradition are asked: "What is justification? A. Justification is an act of God's free grace, wherein he pardons all our sins (Rom. 3:24; Eph. 1:7), and accepts us as righteous in his sight (2 Cor. 5:21) only for the righteousness of Christ imputed to us (Rom. 5:19), and received by faith alone (Gal. 2:16; Phil. 3:9)."[12] So it goes.

---

10. COC 3:114.
11. COC 3:744.
12. Spurgeon, Catech. Q32

6. Anglican Tradition

The Ten Articles of 1536 state: "All bishops and preachers shall instruct and teach our people committed by us to their spiritual charge, that this word justification signifies remission of our sins and our acceptation or reconciliation into the grace and favor of God, that is to say, our perfect renovation in Christ" (Article 5, par. 1).[13] Nothing different here.

Justification refers to "the gratuitous promises of the Gospel, to the comfort of our own souls; whereby we lay hold of Christ with all his benefits, having an earnest trust and confidence in God, that he will be merciful unto us for his only Son's sake. So that a true believer may be certain, by the assurance of faith, of the forgiveness of his sins, and of his everlasting salvation by Christ" (Irish Articles, 1615, art. 8, par. 37).[14]

7. Wesleyan Traditions

Wesley's Standard Sermon on Justification by Faith sets forth the classic Reformation teaching of justification, the verdict expressed in God the Son's self-sacrificing action on the cross (Homily #5 1746 B1:181-99 J#5 V:53-64). Into the fallen human condition God sends his Son as a sacrifice for the sins of the world. God the Son on the cross is embodying an incomparable word of divine pardon, apart from any act or merit of our own, which invites us to be reconciled again to the Father and brought back into our original condition of holiness and happiness. This reconciling act of God is our justification, our being uprighted in the presence of God, not by anything we have done on our own but by what God has done for us on the cross. The sinner is uprighted by atoning grace declared on the cross, by God's own righteousness which is the work of Christ for us, a juridical act that occurs through an event, the cross. As in Adam, "the common father and representative of us all," death passed upon all men, "even so, by the sacrifice for sin made by the second Adam, as the representative of us all, God is so far reconciled to the world, that He hath given them a new covenant" (J. Wesley, Standard Sermons, #5, i.5-9, 1:185-87). Saving faith is our trusting response to this divine deed of justification in which we are

13. DER 170.
14. DER 443-44.

counted righteous. God the Spirit works in the heart to transform our behavior so that it bears fruits.

This is not the place to waste ink and trees trying to prove that all these documents quoted are official teaching in various Christian communions. Anyone who does not know that the Westminster Confession is dear to Reformed believers just does not know Calvinism. Anyone who does not know that the 25 Articles are doctrinal standards for most of the Wesleyan tradition does not know that tradition.

8. Pentecostal Traditions

The Statement of Faith of the Assemblies of God Theological Seminary, Springfield, Missouri, affirms simply: "We believe the only means of being cleansed from sin is through repentance and faith in the precious blood of Christ." The Statement of Fundamental Truths of the Assemblies of God has a more explicit article on salvation which states: "Man's only hope of redemption is through the shed blood of Jesus Christ the Son of God. Conditions to Salvation: Salvation is received through repentance toward God and faith toward the Lord Jesus Christ. By the washing of regeneration and renewing of the Holy Ghost, being justified by grace through faith, man becomes an heir of God according to the hope of eternal life (Luke 24:47; John 3:3; Romans 10:13-15; Ephesians 2:8; Titus 2:11; 3:5-7)." Another Pentecostal affirmation of classic justification teaching is the Basis of Union (1979, 2.3): "We believe and teach and firmly maintain the Scriptural doctrine of justification (Rom. 5:1). We believe also that Jesus Christ shed His blood for the complete cleansing of the justified believer from all indwelling sin, and from its pollution subsequent to regeneration" (Pentecostal Fire-Baptized Holiness Church).

Many prominent Pentecostal leaders have been signatories to recent consensual evangelical formulations of justification teaching in such documents as the Amsterdam Declaration (2000), The Gospel of Jesus Christ, An Evangelical Celebration (1999), The Manila Manifesto (1988), and the Lausanne Covenant (1974). Although some points of doctrine in those documents were debated among Pentecostals, very little disagreement was noted on the consensual doctrine of justification that they with one voice expressed.

9. *Arguing Consensuality*

What we still have ahead of us is demonstrating that this same teaching of justification was profoundly and thoroughly understood a thousand years before the Reformation.

Is there a consensually received pre-Protestant Catholic-Orthodox doctrine of justification that can be textually documented? Can evangelicals and liberals and Pentecostals and Catholics all talk about salvation using the same scripture texts and a shared history of classic scripture teaching that was firmly established long before the sixteenth-century Council of Trent or the Augsburg Confession?

At this point, the evangelical habit is to say: Hold on! Let's not forget the differences. Then follows a rehearsal of sixteenth-century issues between Protestants and Catholics from Mary to purgatory, from relics to papal authority. My purpose is to show a consensus on justification teaching that preceded these differences.

My purpose is to demonstrate consensuality. The best and only way to do that is to quote comparatively the authoritative doctrinal teachers of various Christian communions. While there may be slight differences of language among them, there is an astonishing similarity of substantive biblical reasoning among them.

All parties have a duty to look at the evidence both for changes in outlook since the sixteenth century and a consensus that prevailed a millennium before these differences. Protestants are correct to remember the importance of these historic differences, but not to the extent that they ignore or preclude recognition of the deeper historic consensus of Pauline exegesis that preceded these differences by a thousand years.

Both Protestant and secular accounts of the last four centuries have focused on the development and accentuation of differences. What we have not heard adequately argued is the underlying continuity that truly persists from patristic to Reformation, revivalist, modern, charismatic, and Pentecostal views of salvation. If this were already recognized, there would be no need for this book. This patristic-Protestant consensus is the proper textual basis for proceeding today to rediscover the deeper hidden unity of the body of Christ.

B. Introducing Locus Classicus
Patristic Texts on Justification

Out of an abundance of patristic texts on justification, I have selected a few typical examples from the East and a few from the West to show exemplary expressions of clear, explicit pre-Protestant, authentically Pauline justification teaching.

1. Early Eastern Voices on Justification

Key textual evidences from Origen, John Chrysostom, and Theodoret of Cyrrhus show that leading eastern patristic writers anticipated standard classic Reformation teaching on justification:

The leading biblical interpreter from the great school of Antioch, Theodoret of Cyrrhus, in his fourth-century commentary on the Epistles of Paul, reflected on Ephesians 2:8, "For by grace you have been saved through faith," in this way: "All we bring to grace is our faith. But even in this faith, divine grace itself has become our enabler. For [Paul] adds, 'And this is not of yourselves but it is a gift of God; not of works, lest anyone should boast (Eph. 2:8-9).' It is not of our own accord that we have believed, but we have come to belief after having been called; and even when we had come to believe, He did not require of us purity of life, but approving mere faith, God bestowed on us forgiveness of sins" (Interpretation of the Fourteen Epistles of Paul).[15] A thousand years before Luther.

A generation before Theodoret, John Chrysostom had expressly stated: "So that you may not be elated by the magnitude of these benefits, see how Paul puts you in your place. For 'by grace you are saved,' he says, 'through faith.' Then, so as to do no injury to free will, he allots a role to us, then takes it away again, saying 'and this not of ourselves.' . . . Even faith, he says, is not from us. For if the Lord had not come, if he had not called us, how should we have been able to believe? 'For how,' [Paul] says, 'shall they believe if they have not heard?' (Rom. 10:14). So even the act of faith is not self-initiated. It is, he says, 'the gift of God' (Eph. 2:8c)." So writes

---

15. FEF 3:248-49,* sec. 2163.

Chrysostom at the end of the fourth century (Hom. on Ephesians 2.8).[16] Luther conserved this previous tradition.

In asking why boasting is excluded, Origen commented on Romans 3:28, "For we hold that a man is justified by faith apart from works of law." "If an example is required," remarked Origen, "I think it must suffice to mention the thief on the cross, who asked Christ to save him and was told: 'Truly, this day you will be with me in paradise' (Luke 23:43). . . . A man is justified by faith. The works of the law can make no contribution to this. Where there is no faith which might justify the believer, even if there are works of the law these are not based on the foundation of faith. Even if they are good in themselves they cannot justify the one who does them, because faith is lacking, and faith is the mark of those who are justified by God" (Commentary on the Epistle to the Romans).[17] So was justification by faith alone understood before the Reformers? The texts make this undeniable. These examples make it clear that justification teaching was rightly understood among the eastern patristic writers in a way that classic Reformation writers would have every reason to respect. But what of the West? Equally strong in these points.

2. Early Western Voices on Justification

Key texts from the West by Clement of Rome, Augustine, Prosper, and Fulgentius demonstrate patristic anticipations of Reformation teaching on justification, in substantial agreement with the East.

The earliest of Paul's interpreters, Clement of Rome, 95 A.D., in his Letter to the Corinthians (32:4, 33:1), clearly struck to the root of justification teaching: "We, therefore, who have been called by His will in Christ Jesus, are not justified by ourselves, neither by our wisdom or understanding or piety, nor by the works we have wrought in holiness of heart, but by the faith by which almighty God has justified all men from the beginning, to whom be glory forever and ever. Amen. What, then, shall we do, brethren? Shall we cease from good works, and shall we put an end to love? May the Master forbid that such should ever happen among us; rather let us be eager to perform every good work earnestly and willingly."[18] Here Paul's

16. IOEP 2:160; ACCS NT 8:134.
17. CER 2.132, 134, 136; ACCS NT 6:104.
18. FEF 1:9, sec. 16.

preaching is appropriated: we are justified by a faith that becomes active in love. Writing in Greek, but living in Rome, Clement can be counted as a voice from either the East or West, as can Irenaeus.

Augustine followed this same tendency of interpretation that would later appear in Luther. In his letter (186, 3, 10) to Paulinus of Nola, Augustine subtly analyzed the relation of grace and freedom: "Let no one say to himself: 'If [justification] is from faith, how is it freely given? (cf. Rom. 3:24): If faith merits it, why is it not rather paid than given?' Let the faithful man not say such a thing; for, if he says: 'I have faith, therefore I merit justification,' he will be answered: 'What have you that you did not receive?' (1 Cor. 4:7). If, therefore, faith entreats and receives justification, according as God has apportioned to each in the measure of his faith (Rom. 12:3), nothing of human merit precedes the grace of God, but grace itself merits increase . . . with the will accompanying but not leading, following along but not going in advance."[19]

We have repeatedly been told by the liberal tradition following Harnack that the ancient Christian writers had no such awareness of justification by grace through faith. Yet there it lies in the texts. "Grace is given, not because we have done good works, but in order that we may have power to do them, not because we have fulfilled the Law, but in order that we may be able to fulfill it" (Augustine, The Spirit and the Letter).[20]

Prosper of Aquitaine in his Call of All Nations (1, 17) stated the doctrine in much the same way Luther would later: "And just as there are no crimes so detestable that they can prevent the gift of grace, so too there can be no works so eminent that they are owed in condign judgement that which is given freely. Would it not be a debasement of redemption in Christ's blood, and would not God's mercy be made secondary to human works, if justification, which is through grace, were owed in view of preceding merits, so that it were not the gift of a Donor, but the wages of a laborer?"[21] Hence it is incorrect to presume that patristic teaching knew nothing of justification.

That this faith constantly becomes active in love, according to the early Christian exegetes, is evident from this passage from Fulgentius of Ruspe who wrote in The Rule of Faith (1): "Without faith it is impossible

19. FEF 3:10, sec. 1446.
20. LCC 8:206.
21. FEF 3:195, sec. 2044.

to please God (Heb. 11:6). For faith is the basis of all goods. Faith is the beginning of human salvation. Without faith no one can pertain to the number of the sons of God, because without it neither will anyone obtain the grace of justification in this life nor possess eternal life in the future; and if anyone does not walk now in faith, he will not arrive at the actuality. Without faith every human labor is empty."[22]

Next we will take one scripture passage alone, Ephesians 2, and limit comments to those made by the early Christian scripture scholars.

3. A Case in Point: Consensual Interpretation of Ephesians 2

Ephesians 2:4-10 is the cardinal text through which Luther and Calvin argued for justification by grace through faith. It says: "But God, who is rich in mercy, out of the great love with which he loved us, even when we were dead through our trespasses, made us alive together with Christ (by grace you are saved), and raised us up with him, and made us sit with him in the heavenly places with Christ Jesus, that in the coming ages he might show the immeasurable riches of his grace in kindness toward us in Christ Jesus. For by grace you have been saved through faith; and this is not your own doing, it is the gift of God — not because of works, lest any man should boast. For we are his workmanship, created in Christ Jesus for good works, which God prepared beforehand, that we should walk in them."

Luther understood that we are saved while yet sinners; so did Ambrosiaster in the fourth century. "All thanksgiving for our salvation is to be given only to God. He extends his mercy to us so as to recall us to life precisely while we are straying, without looking for the right road. And thus we are not to glory in ourselves but in God, who has regenerated us by a heavenly birth through faith in Christ" (Epistle to the Ephesians).[23]

"We are his workmanship" (Eph. 2:10), owing everything to him. Wrote Jerome: "We are his creation. This means that it is from him that we live, breathe, understand and are able to believe, because he is the One who made us. And note carefully that he did not say 'we are his fashioning and molding,' but 'we are his creation.' Molding starts with the mud of the

---

22. FEF 3:295, sec. 2260.

23. Luther, *Commentary on Paul's Epistles*, ed. K. J. Vogels, 1968, CSEL 81.3:82; ACCS NT 8:134.

earth, but creation from the outset is 'according to the image and likeness of God'" (Gen. 1:26-27; Epistle to the Ephesians 1.2.10).[24]

In the mid-fourth century Marius Victorinus commented on Ephesians 2: "The fact that you Ephesians are saved is not something that comes from yourselves. It is the gift of God. It is not from your works, but it is God's grace and God's gift, not from anything you have deserved" (Epistle to the Ephesians 1.2.9).[25]

Jerome argued that no one can earn grace. "We are saved by grace rather than works, for we can give God nothing in return for what he has bestowed on us" (Epistle to the Ephesians 1.2.1).[26]

Ambrosiaster taught that God is first mercifully seeking us before we seek his mercy. "These are the true riches of God's mercy, that even when we did not seek it mercy was made known through his own initiative" (Epistle to the Ephesians 2.4)[27] — standard Reformation teaching found already in the fourth century.

We do not deserve this gift of salvation. "He did not make us deserving, since we did not receive things by our own merit but by the grace and goodness of God" (Marius Victorinus, Epistle to the Ephesians 1.2.7).[28]

Faith itself is a gift of God. Without it no one is saved. "The blessed Paul argues that we are saved by faith, which he declares to be not from us but a gift from God. Thus there cannot possibly be true salvation where there is no true faith, and, since this faith is divinely enabled, it is without doubt bestowed by his free generosity. Where there is true belief through true faith, true salvation certainly accompanies it. Anyone who departs from true faith will not possess the grace of true salvation" (Eph. 2:7; Fulgentius, On the Incarnation 1).[29] Neither Luther nor Calvin stated it more forcefully.

The logic of Ephesians 2, according to the Fathers, is this: We are mercifully saved despite our unworthiness, through the resurrection of Christ. Without exception, all who are saved are saved by grace. The faithful are already in a sense raised through the resurrection of Christ, and hence are called to live a new life. Christians are not arrogant when they

24. PL 26:470B-C (577); ACCS NT 8:134.
25. BT 1972:152 (1256A-B); ACCS NT 8:134.
26. PL 26:468B (574); ACCS NT 8:132.
27. CSEL 81.3:80; ACCS NT 8:131.
28. BT 1972:152 (1255C); ACCS NT 8:132.
29. CCL 91:313; ACCS NT 8:133-34.

celebrate this salvation, since their faith, though a unique means of salvation, is not a work but is shaped by divine grace. We can claim no credit for our conversion, or any subsequent good works. We can and must do works, but have no right to glory in them or in ourselves. Although we now fail to do good works, God prepares both present and future works for us, in which we must persevere.[30]

4. Whether These Voices Harmonize: Modest Objectives on Doctrinal Concurrence

According to these texts, which only scratch the surface, Luther's and Calvin's justification teaching was profoundly anticipated both in eastern and western patristic writers. Luther rightly viewed his task not as an original invention of new doctrine, but as the recovery of classic orthodox Pauline justification teaching. These typical excerpts can be profusely multiplied.

But I am hearing objections: Are there not patristic references that deny the Reformers' views? Is there a viable consensus either among the patristic writers or the Reformers? How is a consensus established? Who is to say what the consensus is? Was the voice of orthodoxy not merely a matter of political power? What about exceptions to the alleged consensus? Even if there were a body of literature to which Protestants, Catholics, and Orthodox can assent, isn't the depth of their modern alienation such that mere texts cannot overcome their differences? Does the examination of ancient texts really have any implication for our prayers for greater proximate unity in the body of Christ today? Hasn't liberal modern ecumenics become so distant from classic orthodoxy that evangelical ecumenics should leave it behind and give up on despairing attempts? These are among the questions we hope to address in the pages ahead.

For now, I have two modest preliminary responses:

First, even if I cannot convince all readers that there is a full-orbed patristic consensus on justification that is virtually indistinguishable from the Reformers' teaching, at least I can establish the point clearly that there are in patristic texts clear anticipations of the Reformers' teaching of justification — that will be undeniable because I will show that these texts ex-

---

30. I am indebted to Mark Edwards of Christ Church, Oxford, editor of volume 8 of the *Ancient Christian Commentary on Scripture*, for many of the new translations herein.

ist! So one modest objective will be accomplished: It will no longer be possible hereafter to say that the Fathers had no developed notion or doctrine of justification by grace through faith.

Second, in establishing point one, the ball now is in the court of the defenders of the exclusiveness and uniqueness of the Reformers' teaching. It is now incumbent upon them to show textually how the patristic teaching of justification differs substantially from the Reformers. This, I believe, will be very difficult to prove.

C. God's Costly Way of Reestablishing
a Right Relation with the Sinner

1. Comparing Old and New Testament
Interpretations of Justification

In the New Testament, as in the Old, to justify is to vindicate an action as right in God's presence. It is to stand in a right relation with God.

In the cross there is provided an entirely different way of standing upright in God's presence than that provided under the law.

Precisely amid the history of sin, good news has come: one may come into a right relation with God by being "justified freely by his grace" through faith in Christ (Rom. 3:24; Calvin, Catechism of Church of Geneva).[31]

2. Old Testament Anticipations

The Old Testament already provides us with startling and profound anticipations of "uprighting by grace." Even as early as Abel some had come to know that one may stand upright before God by grace through faith, for "By faith he [Abel] was commended as a righteous man" (Heb. 11:4). So also did Noah become "heir of the righteousness that comes by faith" (Heb. 11:7).

Abraham was the decisive type: "By faith Abraham, when called to go to a place he would later receive as his inheritance, obeyed and went, even

31. LCC 12:103-7.

though he did not know where he was going" (Heb. 11:8). His faith "was credited [accounted] to him as righteousness" (Gen. 15:6; Rom. 4:3).[32] Habakkuk grasped the heart of the matter, that "the righteous will live by his faith" (2:4).[33]

The prophet Isaiah clearly saw that a right relation with God would come through the suffering of the messianic Servant who "through the Lord makes his life a guilt offering," who "after the suffering of his soul . . . he will see the light of life, and be satisfied; by his knowledge my righteous servant will justify many, and he will bear their iniquities" (Isa. 53:10, 11).

This Expected One appeared in Jesus, who announced the coming righteousness of God, and himself embodied that coming. Those who enter his kingdom, where God's own righteousness personally comes and reigns, participate in a righteousness that exceeds that of the scribes and Pharisees (Matt. 5:20).

In his presence even the tax-collector, grieving over his sins, could "go home justified" (Luke 18:14). Those who pretend to merit righteousness or desperately justify themselves in resistance to the coming of God's freely forgiving love are not ready for this kingdom of grace (Luke 10:29; 16:15). The righteous (δίκαιοι) are those who offer acts of compassion to the needy neighbor, yet even in doing so may remain unaware until the last day that the living God is incognito in the neighbor (Matt. 25:37, 46).

3. Why Do We So Fiercely Resist Hearing This Good News?

We in our self-assertiveness would much prefer to justify ourselves rather than receive God's free gift. So it is characteristic of the fallen, pride-driven human condition that we continue to seek to justify ourselves by our own individual works and righteousness, instead of receiving it as a gift.

Sex role assumptions play heavily into modern forms of works-righteousness. Women often try to justify themselves by their beauty or attractiveness or nurturing abilities. Men more often justify their existence by their prowess or productivity, their athletic ability or wealth.

The message of justification is difficult to accept because it seems too good to be true. It says: Stop trying to justify yourself. You do not need to.

32. Calvin, Inst. 3.11.
33. Cf. JD 13.

There is no way to buy or deserve God's love or acceptance. You are already being offered God's love on the cross without having to jump hoops or pass tests. You are already there, where you think you are not.

4. While You Were Yet Ungodly

The word of the cross is not: "I will love you *if* you become perfect," but "While we were yet sinners, at the right time, Christ died for the ungodly" (Rom. 5:6-8).

Luther understood this profoundly. On the basis of the self-justifying works of the law, the holy God would not let sin go unpunished. Yet on the basis of the gospel, God is merciful precisely toward humbled sinners.[34]

Origen grasped it just as clearly in the third century. "Christ died not for the godly but for the ungodly. For we were ungodly before we turned to God, and Christ died for us before we believed. Undoubtedly he would not have done this unless either he himself, or God the Father, who gave up his only-begotten Son for the redemption of the ungodly, had superabundant love towards us" (Origen, Commentary on the Epistle to the Romans).[35] "By saying that Christ died for us while we were yet sinners, Paul gives us hope that we will be saved through him, much more so now that we are cleansed from sin and justified against the wrath which remains for sinners" (Origen, Commentary on the Epistle to the Romans).[36]

"Christ died for the ungodly. Now if someone will hardly die for a righteous man, how can it be that someone should die for ungodly people? And if someone might dare to die for one good man, (or not dare, since the phrase is ambiguous), how can it be that someone would dare to die for a multitude of the ungodly?" (Ambrosiaster, Commentary on Paul's Epistles).[37]

In one of the decisive passages on grace, Paul wrote in Romans 10:20-21: "Then Isaiah is so bold as to say: 'I have been found by those who did not seek me; I have shown myself to those who did not ask for me.' But of Israel he says: 'All day long I have held out my hands to a disobedient and contrary people.'" According to Diodore, this passage anticipates the com-

---

34. Luther, Lectures on Romans, LW 25.
35. CER 2:280, 282; ACCS NT 6:131.
36. CER 2:288; ACCS NT 6:132.
37. CSEL 81:157; ACCS NT 6:131-32.

ing servant Messiah: "It appears from the holding out of his hands that God is calling the people to himself. It is also a sign pointing toward the form of the cross" (Diodore of Tarsus, Pauline Commentary from the Greek Church).[38] The point: we are found by grace in the sheltering cross, even before we seek it. Commented Jerome: "The hands of the Lord lifted up to heaven were not begging for help, but were sheltering us, his miserable creatures" (Jerome, Sermons 68).[39]

Thus the Fathers agree: We are found by God's mercy *before* we seek him.

D. How Divine Love Brings Sinners into an Uprighted Relation with Divine Justice

The heart of the gospel idea of uprighting (justification) cannot be penetrated without pursuing carefully the metaphor of a courtroom verdict.

1. Unpacking the Courtroom Metaphor

Many crucial biblical terms describing our salvation come directly out of the setting of the court. Justification is such a term. It belongs with other judicial terms like judge, pardon, sentence, and verdict. These are sometimes called forensic or juridical metaphors.

God's justifying verdict is compared to a judicial act by which God declares the sinner free from guilt — acquitted! The Judge forgives the one who repents and believes in the unique way the Judge has provided for the sinner's release. On the basis of this pardon, the person is declared right in the presence of the divine Judge.

God acquits the ungodly who believe in Christ, and declares them just. Condemned before, they are now released. Previously rejected, they are now accepted personally *(acceptatio personae)*[40] into the presence of the holy God. The expected sure condemnation has been unexpectedly reversed into a complete, unambiguous acquittal.

38. NTA 15:102; ACCS NT 6:283.
39. FC 57:83; ACCS NT 6:283.
40. Melanchthon, LCC 19:88ff.; cf. CR XXI.742.

53

2. The Judge and the Law

In this court, God is judge, whose judgments are undeniably right and sure (Gen. 18:25). The law is the expression of what God requires. The law brings into expression under historical conditions what God demands. God's law does not change as history changes, but our perceptions of it change, as we are able to discern it through the history of God's self-disclosure.

God is not responsible to some law that stands above God. Rather, God gives the law. God is not subservient to a moral law that precedes God. Nothing precedes God. Rather, the origin of all right law and upright living is in the righteous One alone. The righteousness of God is the basis for whatever degree of righteousness the law is able to convey.

Through the law, God is calling rational creatures to act in a way that corresponds to God's own goodness and holiness. God is calling those made in God's image to act in a way that mirrors the righteousness of God. This occurs precisely within the limits of the history of sin.

God wants us to act in a benevolent way because God is incomparably benevolent, to act justly because God is incomparably just. God asks us to act fairly and mercifully because God is incomparably fair and merciful. It is in this law, this divine requirement, that the faithful "delight" and "meditate day and night" (Ps. 1:2).

3. Elements of the Courtroom Drama

All the elements of the courtroom situation are presupposed in salvation teaching: The judge is God: "You have come to God, the judge of all" (Heb. 12:23). The defendant is I and everyone else who has become enmeshed in the history of sin. "The whole world" is being "held accountable to God" (Rom. 3:19). The plaintiff or accuser is personified as Moses, or generalized as "the law": "Your accuser is Moses" (John 5:45).

The internal witness is conscience, the moral testimony of the heart, or moral reasoning: "the requirements of the law are written on their hearts," "their consciences also bearing witness, and their thoughts now accusing, now even defending them" (Rom. 2:15).

In this court an indictment is being read according to "the written code, with its regulations, that was against us and that stood opposed to us" (Col. 2:14). A sentence is being delivered: "Indeed, in our hearts we felt the sentence of death" (2 Cor. 1:9). The defendant is as good as dead: "As for you, you were dead in your transgressions and sins" (Eph. 2:1).

4. Our Advocate

In this courtroom an incomparable Advocate has appeared. "We have one who speaks to the Father in our defense — Jesus Christ, the Righteous One" (1 John 2:1). A satisfaction is offered, substituting another's suffering for the penalty due to sinners: "He is the atoning sacrifice for our sins" (1 John 2:2). The sacrifice of one is accepted for many: "Through the obedience of the one man the many will be made righteous" (Rom. 5:19).

On this basis the judge reverses the judgment, grants a full acquittal, and justifies the accused: "Therefore, there is now no condemnation for those who are in Christ Jesus" (Rom. 8:1). The sinless One has become sin for us, taking punishment on our behalf, so that we might live to him.

5. How Clemency Comes Late in the Trial

There are three moments in ordinary court procedure in which it is possible for a defendant to be declared justified or not culpable. First, the Judge can dismiss the case upon arraignment if it can be shown clearly by the facts that the defendant is not guilty. But this is not the case for us, for we are guilty. Second, after arraignment, even if the evidence is damaging, the law itself may protect one from penalty, and thus one may be justified or declared right in relation to the law. But after this arraignment, it becomes all the more clear that we are guilty and deserve condemnation. Third, at the very conclusion of a trial in which one already is found guilty, one may be accounted upright by executive clemency, wherein the penalty may be remitted on the principle of *pardon*.

It is in this third sense, at this late and final, dramatic stage of the trial, that the New Testament most often employs the courtroom metaphor of justification. For all are guilty as charged of sin (before and after arraignment), hence there is no other ground left except unmerited divine clemency. Such clemency does not imply an abrogation of the law, but a more profound fulfillment of the law by exercising a judicial prerogative, which only the Judge can do. The law has not been circumvented or ignored, but fulfilled through a substitute punishment. The law is being personally applied to a particular case by a particular Judge as a decision rightly and reasonably made, in which the law itself is vindicated, reestablished, and magnified.

The Judge's decision to "account as righteous" comes as the very last event of reversal on the last day in this extended courtroom drama called history. This reversal is confirmed finally on the last day, but that last day is anticipated in the cross. The judicial decision depends for its context and meaning upon the previous events of transgression, arrest, charge, evidentiary presentation, and judgment.

It is amid this metaphorical theater that the biblical terms are understood: δικαίωσις is a judicial decision or sentence of acquittal; δίκαιος, (righteous), δικαίωμα (judgment), δικαιόω (to declare righteous, to justify), λογίζομαι (to reckon or credit the account of), and δικαιοσύνη (righteousness) all derive from the same judicial premise.

Such terms are not applied flatly or literally or univocally, but analogically as an attempt of limited human speech to do approximate justice to God's actual declarative action of pardon that occurred on the cross. Analogies express intuitive similarities amid remaining differences. Such analogies are not equations or mathematical correlations or statements of fact. Rather, they represent through human language a divine verdict that actually occurred in a particular historical event, the cross. God's righteousness cannot be reduced to human concepts of righteousness. It is known through an event. So God's justifying act of accounting the sinner righteous in Christ is best viewed not simplistically as a literal, bare, banal, uninterpretable fact. Rather, it is an event interpreted copiously under the subtle and delicate laws of analogy.

6. The Acquittal

The salvation event is thus compared to an act of acquittal: The defendant is instantly relieved of all charges. It is that act by which the court officially declares one to stand upright in the presence of the final Judge.

Love covers a multitude of sins. Justification is full pardon from all guilt and a new reckoning of the sinner as righteous (Epistle to Diognetus,

9).[41] As in a court of law you may be declared released from all charges, so in the presence of God you may be declared righteous so that your sin no longer counts against you.

The bare metaphor of acquittal, taken abstractly, is insufficient to express the full extent of God's saving action. There is a difference: Acquittal may imply that one has *done no wrong*. Instead, justification (remarkably!) is the acceptance of the sinner, united in Christ by faith, precisely while it remains clear that he or she has indeed *done wrong*. It is just while the conscience-stricken sinner is disclaiming his innocence and openly declaring his guilt, that acquittal is announced. If such a condemned person is to be delivered from guilt, it must be by a just cancellation of the charge or blotting out from the record any charge against him.

7. There Is Now No Condemnation

Justification is best understood in direct contrast with condemnation. Those justified are not condemned. Those not justified are condemned. There is no middle way (Matt. 12:37), no way to stand as partially justified. To justify is to liberate totally and once for all the offender precisely while condemnation seemed just. Under the law the sinner is condemned. Under the gospel the sinner is justified. "It is God who justifies. Who is he that condemns?" (Rom. 8:33, 34).

Gospel justification views the convicted offender as suddenly and fully pardoned in a way that destroys the connection between his behavior and its penal consequence (Apology of the Augsburg Confession).[42] Pardon reverses the sentence of condemnation (Rom. 8:1). Forgiveness is not cheap. It is not as if the sinner is inaccurately declared innocent without any price being paid. Rather, the price is paid by another, so that the liability to punishment of the sinner is removed. "Justification is the forgiveness of sins (cf. Rom. 3:23-25; Acts 3:19; Luke 18:14), liberation from the dominating power of sin and death (Rom. 5:12-21) and from the curse of the law (Gal. 3:10-14)" (JD 13).

Luther was not the first to discover the power of this reversal. Anselm

41. ECW, p. 180.
42. BOC, pp. 100ff.

wrote that even if God "shall say that you are a sinner, you say: 'Lord, I interpose the death of our Lord Jesus Christ between my sins and you.'"[43]

And before Anselm, the very early Epistle of Barnabas, 5, argued that the atoning cross is the event that enables our pardon and salvation: "For to this end the Lord endured to deliver up His flesh to corruption, that we might be sanctified through the remission of sins, which is effected by His blood of sprinkling."[44]

This is why justification can be offered to sinners only. Those who assume they are not sinners assume they do not need it. They need not apply.

8. Behavioral Righteousness Distinguished from Juridical Righteousness

The imputation of the righteousness of Christ does not depend upon personal or behavioral righteousness, but on faith alone. No one possesses righteousness before God as an acquired human virtue. In faith we are antecedently justified (i.e., before any of our works), and consequently called to live out our antecedent justification by grace alone.

Protestant doctrine is aware that an evangelical response of personal righteousness is enabled and called for as a response to the gospel. It is believers who are called "righteous" due to their faith. But this is not in reference to an independently based habituation of righteousness, as if the habit of doing what pleases God might become itself an acquired human virtue that might be called the righteousness of God, so that human acts eclipse God's gift.

Justification in its biblical sense does not imply that one is already behaviorally or in practice ethically made perfectly righteous, but rather regarded so in the presence of God. It means to declare or deem upright so as to acquit from guilt and punitive liability in such a way as to invite, permit, and enable a full human response to sufficient grace.[45] It is not an act by which the sinner's deportment or conduct is already or immediately or subjectively made outwardly righteous. Scripture does not characteristically use the term "justify" to imply the direct infusion of a fully matured,

43. Liber meditationum, Consolatio, PL 158:687.
44. ANF 1:139.
45. Calvin, Inst. 3.11-14; TDNT, δικαίωσις.

fully habituated behavioral quality into the recipient. Rather, it refers to an actual and legitimized declaration through which one is accredited right before the law and Lawgiver.

This is clear by analogy with Christ's seeming "sin" which is his real act of becoming "sin for us," a substitutional or forensic "sinfulness" on our behalf (Chrysostom, Homilies on the Epistles of Paul to the Corinthians 11.5).[46] Christ had no sin ethically, but being truly God, truly human, became sin for us in a substitutionary sense, so that we might share really in God's righteousness. Our righteousness does not imply an already actualized or perfectly just ethical behavior.

Hence the Irish Articles of Religion of 1615 (Art. 35) summarize: "Thus the justice and mercy of God do embrace each other: the grace of God not shutting out the justice of God in the matter of our justification, but only shutting out the justice of man (that is to say, the justice of our own works) from being any cause of our deserving our justification."[47]

These texts sufficiently define justification. Now defined, how is it received?

46. NPNF 1 12:333-35.
47. COC 3:432-33.

CHAPTER THREE

Receiving Righteousness from God

Patristic texts abound in justification teaching. What follows is a brief account of key patristic texts on expiation, substitutionary sacrifice, punitive liability, and God's revealed righteousness.[1]

A. Justified by His Blood

The Fathers treat justification by showing clearly how Christ is "made to be sin for us." We receive righteousness from God, being "justified by his blood." The Fathers thoroughly explicated the meaning of sacrificial blood, and expiation as an exchange of punitive liability. The substitutionary language so familiar in Protestant atonement teaching is richly utilized in the Fathers' extensive comments on biblical texts dealing with redemption, ransom, slavery to sin, and substitutionary sacrifice.

1. In What Sense Is Christ "Made to Be Sin for Us"?

Christ knew no sin, but he was made sin for us. This occurred by the imputation of our sin to him. The key text is 2 Corinthians 5:21: "For our sake he

1. For a fuller presentation of many additional patristic comments on justification, I refer the reader to New Testament volumes 6, 7, 8, 9, and 11 of the *Ancient Christian Commentary on Scripture*, variously edited by Gerald Bray, Peter Gorday, and Mark Edwards, to whom I am grateful for some of the new translations that follow.

made him to be sin who knew no sin, so that in him we might become the righteousness of God." It was central to the Fathers' justification teaching.

Christ was not a sinner, but a victim for sinners, according to Cyril of Alexandria: "We do not say that Christ became a sinner, far from it, but being righteous (or rather righteousness, because he did not know sin at all), the Father made him a victim for the sins of the world" (Letter 41.10).[2]

Christ knew no sin either inwardly or outwardly, either in intention or action. Yet he was voluntarily made to be sin for us by the imputation of our sin to him.

John Chrysostom explained: "God allowed his Son to suffer as if a condemned sinner, so that we might be delivered from the penalty of our sins. This is God's righteousness, that we are not justified by works (for then they would have to be perfect, which is impossible), but by grace, in which case all our sin is removed" (Homilies on the Epistles of Paul to the Corinthians 11:5).[3]

The Fathers teach that Christ was made an offering for our sins. "It was only because all flesh was subject to sin that he was made sin for us. In view of the fact that he was made an offering for sins, it is not wrong for him to be said to have been made 'sin,' because in the law the sacrifice which was offered for sins used to be called a 'sin.' After his death on the cross Christ descended to hell, because it was death, working through sin, which gave hell its power. Christ defeated death by his death, and brought such benefit to sinners that now death cannot hold those who are marked with the sign of the cross" (Ambrosiaster, Commentary on Paul's Epistles).[4]

The assumption is that Christ is fully human in taking on our human curse, yet without sin. "This proves that his body and soul are of the same substance as ours" (Ambrose, The Sacrament of the Incarnation of our Lord 7.76),[5] yet without sin. Theodoret summarized: "Christ was called what we are in order to call us to be what he is" (Commentary on the Second Epistle to the Corinthians 318).[6]

Later the Protestant confessions would echo the same apostolic teaching: "He who knew no sin was made sin for us, that we might be made the righteousness of God in him. He bore our sins in his own body.

2. FC 76:174; ACCS NT 7:252.
3. NPNF 1 12:334; ACCS NT 7:252.
4. CSEL 81:238; ACCS NT 7:252.
5. FC 44:248; ACCS NT 7:251.
6. PG 82:411; ACCS NT 7:252.

It pleased our heavenly Father, of his infinite mercy, without any desert or deserving, to provide for us the most precious sacrifice of Christ, whereby our ransom might be fully paid, the law fulfilled, and his justice fully satisfied. So that Christ is himself the righteousness of all them that truly do believe in him" (Reformed Episcopal Articles of Religion 1875).[7]

2. Expiation

The Old Testament expiatory figure of the atoning "mercy seat" was explained by Theodoret of Cyrrhus as embracing both priest and lamb: "The mercy seat was gold-plated and placed on top of the ark. On each side was the figure of a cherub. When the high priest approached it, the holy kindness of God was revealed. The apostle teaches us that Christ is the true mercy seat, of which the one in the Old Testament was but a type. The name applies to Christ in his humanity, not in his divinity. For as God Christ responded to the expiation made at the mercy seat. It is as man that he receives this label, just as elsewhere he is called a sheep, a lamb, sin and a curse. Furthermore, the ancient mercy seat was bloodless, because it was inanimate. It could only receive the drops of blood pouring from the sacrificial victims. But the Lord Christ is both God and the mercy seat, both the priest and the lamb, and he performed the work of our salvation by his blood, demanding only faith from us" (Interpretation of the Letter to the Romans).[8] Later confirmed by Protestant teaching, these views were common among the Fathers.

John Chrysostom explained: "Paul calls the redemption an expiation to show that, if the Old Testament type [of sacrifice] had such power, much more did its New Testament counterpart have it. . . . What does it mean 'to show God's righteousness'? It is like declaring his riches not only for him to be rich himself, but also to make others rich. . . . For righteousness is not of works but of faith" (Homilies on Romans, 7).[9]

This expiation "was to prove *at the present time* that he himself is righteous" (Rom. 3:26, italics added). "God allowed all this so that afterward, that is to say in our time, he might show forth his righteousness,"

---

7. Article XII of the Justification of Man, COC 3:818.
8. PG 82 ad loc.; ACCS NT 6:102.
9. NPNF 1 11:378; ACCS NT 6:102.

wrote Origen. "For at the end of the age, in the most recent times, God has manifested his righteousness and given Christ to be our redemption. He has made him our propitiator. If he had sent him as the propitiator at some earlier time, there would have been fewer people whose sins needed propitiating than there are now. For God is just, and therefore he could not justify the unjust. Therefore he required the intervention of a propitiator, so that by having faith in him those who could not be justified by their own works might be justified" (Commentary on the Epistle to the Romans 2:112).[10]

This expiation demonstrated that God "justifies him who has faith in Jesus" (Rom. 3:26). "The present time," explained Ambrosiaster, "means our time, in which God has given what long before he had promised to give at the time at which he gave it. . . . God gave what he promised in order to be revealed as righteous. For he had promised that he would justify those who believe in Christ, as he says in Habakkuk: 'The righteous will live by faith in me' (Hab. 2:4). Whoever has faith in God and Christ is righteous" (Commentary on Paul's Epistles).[11]

3. Justified by His Blood

"Since we have now been justified by his blood, how much more shall we be saved from God's wrath through him" (Rom. 5:9).

"Neither our faith without Christ's blood nor Christ's blood without our faith can justify us. Yet of either of these Christ's blood justifies us much more than our faith. That is why, in my opinion, having said above that we are justified by faith, Paul now says that we are justified by his blood 'much more' (Rom. 5:9)" (Origen, Commentary on the Epistle to the Romans 2:290).[12]

We have been justified by what Christ has done, and not by the way we have responded to him. Our affirmative response merely confirms the value of the gift God has given. Justification is God's work, not man's. It is a decision of the Judge, not of the accused who prior to his pardon is guilty as charged.

10. ACCS NT 6:102-3.
11. CSEL 81 ad loc.; ACCS NT 6:103.
12. ACCS NT 6:132.

4. *Much More Are We Saved by His Blood*

It is this incomparable Anointed One "whom God put forward as an expiation by his blood, to be received by faith. This was to show God's righteousness, because in his divine forbearance he had passed over former sins" (Rom 3.25).

"This expiation was by his blood," wrote Ambrosiaster, which means that "we have been set free by his death so that God might reveal him and condemn death by his passion. This was in order to make his promise clear, by which he set us free from sin as he had promised before. . . . He nullified the sentence by which it seemed just that everyone should be condemned in order to show us that long ago he had decided to liberate the human race, as he promised through Jeremiah the prophet, saying: 'I will forgive their iniquity and I will remember their sin no more' (Jer. 31:34). And in case it might be thought that this promise was for the Jews only, he said through Isaiah: 'My house will be called a house of prayer for all peoples' (Isa. 56:7). For although the promise was made to the Jews, God knew in advance that the ungodly Jews would reject his gift. Therefore he promised that he would allow the Gentiles to share in his grace" (Commentary on Paul's Epistles).[13]

Origen explained the connection between his blood and our redemption in this way: "Although the holy apostle teaches many wonderful things about our Lord Jesus Christ which are said mysteriously about him, in this passage [Rom. 3:25] he has given special prominence to something which, I think, is not readily found in other parts of Scripture. For having just said that Christ gave himself as a redemption for the entire human race so that he might ransom those who were held captive by sin. . . . now he adds something even more sublime, saying that God put him forward 'as an expiation by his blood, to be received by faith.' This means that by the sacrifice of Christ's body God has made expiation on behalf of men and by this has shown his righteousness, in that he forgave their previous sins, which they had committed in the service of the worst possible tyrants. God endured this and allowed these things to happen" (Commentary on the Epistle to the Romans 2:112).[14]

13. CSEL 81 ad loc.; ACCS NT 6:102.
14. ACCS NT 6:101.

5. What Is Redemption?

Origen succinctly explained: "'Redemption' is the word used for what is given to enemies in order to ransom captives and restore them to their liberty. Therefore human beings were held in captivity by their enemies until the coming of the Son of God, who became for us not only the wisdom of God, and righteousness and sanctification (1 Cor. 1:30), but also redemption. He gave himself as our redemption, that is, he surrendered himself to our enemies and poured out his blood on those who were thirsting for it. In this way redemption was obtained for believers" (Origen, Commentary on the Epistle to the Romans 2:110).[15]

6. The Exchange

The apostle's ransom and exchange metaphors were taken as normative as early as the second century Epistle to Diognetus: "He gave His own Son as a ransom for us, the holy One for transgressors, the blameless One for the wicked, the righteous One for the unrighteous, the incorruptible One for the corruptible, the immortal One for them that are mortal. For what other thing was capable of covering our sins than His righteousness? By what other one was it possible that we, the wicked and ungodly, could be justified, than by the only Son of God? O sweet exchange! O unsearchable operation! O benefits surpassing all expectation! that the wickedness of many should be hid in a single righteous One, and that the righteousness of One should justify many transgressors!" (Epistle to Diognetus 9, 2-5).[16]

Later the Protestant Confessions would echo: "He for them paid their ransom, by his death. He for them fulfilled the law, in his life. So that now in him, and by him, every true Christian man may be called a fulfiller of the law" (Reformed Episcopal Articles of Religion 1875).[17]

15. ACCS NT 6:101.
16. ANF 1:28.
17. Article XII of the Justification of Man, COC 3:818.

B. How Righteousness Is Revealed

Righteousness belongs to God. It is revealed in the Gospel. The Gospel reveals already that which is to be finally clarified on the last day. Everything pertaining to righteousness will be revealed on the last day.

1. Righteousness Belongs to God

Romans 3:22-26 summarizes Paul's justification teaching on receiving Christ's righteousness: "This righteousness from God comes through faith in Jesus Christ to all who believe. There is no difference, for all have sinned and fall short of the glory of God, and are justified freely by his grace through the redemption that came by Christ Jesus. God presented him as a sacrifice of atonement, through faith in his blood. He did this to demonstrate his justice, because in his forbearance he had left the sins committed beforehand unpunished — he did it to demonstrate his justice at the present time, so as to be just and the one who justifies those who have faith in Jesus."

God's uprighting of sinners is a common theme of a wide range of scripture texts. Here Paul's teaching is viewed in relation to Mosaic law, the psalms, prophets, and the proclamation of Jesus on righteousness. Chrysostom writes: "This righteousness is not ours but belongs to God, and in saying this, Paul hints to us that it is abundantly available and easy to obtain. For we do not get it by toil and labor but by believing. Then, since his statement does not seem credible, if the adulterer and homosexual, the grave robber and the magician are not only to be suddenly set free from punishment but to be made righteous, and righteous with the righteousness of God, Paul backs up his assertion from the Old Testament (Hab. 2:4). . . . He sends the hearer back to the dispensations of God . . . showing that both the righteous and the sinners were justified by faith even then" (Homilies on Romans 2.17).[18]

Does the continuation of our justification depend on faith alone, or upon our personal righteousness? Justification is completed at once, upon having faith. Believers, upon their justification, are called to complete obedience. The continuation of our pardon, and thereby of a justified state,

---

18. NPNF 1 11:349; ACCS NT 6:32.

depends on the faithfulness of God, upon whose promise we depend. From our side, the continuation of justification depends on faith alone. Nothing is further required except the application of righteousness imputed, that is, faith, taking seriously what God gives. All this occurs in a divine-human relationship, not in a human court or amid human judges. That this is trustable and pleadable before God is known from scripture and from the testimony of all believers.

2. Righteousness Revealed in Creation and Conscience

Even nature shouts out the righteousness of God. The stars declare the height and beauty of God's holiness. "Just as the righteousness of God is revealed in the one who believes, . . . so ungodliness and unrighteousness are revealed in the one who does not believe. From the very structure of heaven it appears that God is angry with them. For this reason he made the stars so beautiful that from them he might be known as their great and wonderful Creator, and alone be adored. It is written in the eighteenth psalm (LXX): 'The heavens declare the glory of God, and the firmament shows his handiwork' (Ps. 19:1), and so the human race is made guilty by the natural law. For men could learn this by the law of nature, with the structure of the world bearing witness that God its author ought alone to be loved, which Moses put down in writing (Deut. 6:5; 10:12; 11:1). But they became ungodly, not worshiping the Creator, and so unrighteousness appeared in them, in that seeing they suppressed the truth, not confessing the one God" (Ambrosiaster, Commentary on Paul's Epistles).[19]

The law of nature known by conscience is distinguished from but consistent with the law revealed to Moses. "The necessary commandments of the Law were taught even by nature. That is, 'You shall not commit adultery, you shall not murder, you shall not steal, you shall not bear false witness against your neighbor, honor your father and mother, and the rest of this kind.' But the commandments about the sabbath and circumcision and lepers and menstruation and sacrifice were peculiar to the [Jewish] law, since nature taught nothing about these matters. These are what he now calls 'works of the law.' The transgression of these is sin, yet the mere

19. CSEL 81:39; ACCS NT 6:35.

keeping of them is not the way of maintaining perfect righteousness" (Theodoret of Cyrrhus, Epistle to the Galatians 2.15-16).[20]

3. Righteousness Revealed in the Gospel

The righteousness of God is now fully made known. "For in the gospel a righteousness from God is revealed, a righteousness that is by faith from first to last, just as it is written: 'The righteous will live by faith'" (Rom. 1:17). The "righteousness from God" means that which has been spoken and accomplished in and through the cross (Calvin, Comm. XX, Rom., 63-6).

"We believe that every one, who through the grace of the Holy Spirit repents and believes the Gospel, confessing and forsaking his sins, and humbly relying upon Christ alone for salvation, is freely pardoned and accepted as righteous in the sight of God, solely on the ground of Christ's perfect obedience and atoning sacrifice" (Presbyterian Church of England, The Articles of the Faith, 1890, Article XIII, Of Justification by Faith).[21] Thus the Reformed tradition confirms the Pauline teaching that was consensually explicated by the Fathers.

4. Giving Account on the Last Day

The concluding act of the justification drama occurs on the last day. This future justifying act of God, having already been established on the cross, is looking toward its final vindication at the end time: "Since we have now been justified by his blood, how much more shall we be saved from God's wrath through him!" (Rom. 5:9). The same word for justification that is used in courts of law (Isa. 5:23; Deut. 25:1) is also used of God's judgment in the last day (Matt. 12:37; Rom. 2:13).

Justification is a presently experienced reality, assuming union with Christ by faith, which anticipates the final day of judgment.

The verdict of this final-day court has already been announced, although ensuing history continues. Justification is an end-time event in

20. CPE 1:340; ACCS NT 8:31.
21. COC 3:918.

which the believer stands already, as if in an anticipative sense. Those united to Christ are justified from all guilt — past, present, and future. Those who die trusting that Christ's righteousness will cover their sins will not be condemned in final judgment, but justified. God's final justifying action awaits the end of history, though the verdict is already known, and celebrated daily in Christian preaching and worship.

Justification on the last day consists of a declaration of righteousness, and an actual admission into glory. There are not two justifications, one by God and another confirmed by our obedience, nor one that occurs with faith, and a final justification that occurs at the end time dependent upon our works. There is only one justification, and that is the one that occurs on the cross. Some teachings of final justification are tempted to ascribe more to our works than to the blood of Christ, more to our obedience than God's own obedience on our behalf.

The final-day character of justification is evident in Jesus' proclamation: "But I tell you that men will have to give account on the day of judgment for every careless word they have spoken. For by your words you will be acquitted, and by your words you will be condemned" (Matt. 12:36, 37). The words by which the faithful are acquitted are a confession of faith in Christ's righteousness. All else is hid in Christ.

C. Our Appropriation of God's Righteousness

Christ is our only righteousness, which we appropriate by faith. Sin is made apparent by the Law. God's own righteousness is revealed in the gospel, works righteousness being rejected, without the moral requirement of God's holiness being overturned. There is no necessity under the gospel to return to Jewish circumcision law. For the heart is now circumcised by faith.

1. Christ Is Our Only Righteousness

Jeremiah prophesied of a coming One who would be called "The Lord our Righteousness" (Jer. 23:6). Paul "proclaims Christ as 'our righteousness' (1 Cor. 1:30), applying to the risen Lord what Jeremiah proclaimed about God himself" (JD 13). Isaiah expected One Anointed to "preach good news to the poor" (Isa. 61:1), who would clothe sinners "with garments of salvation" and array them "in a robe of righteousness" (Isa. 61:10; Chrysostom, Baptismal Instructions).[22] It is he who is attested in Hebrews as "king of righteousness" (Heb. 7:2). Christ is our only righteousness.

The idea that one's sins are unconditionally covered by another's righteousness may, if misunderstood, tend toward license. It is indeed through faith that Christ's righteousness is accounted to us (Rom. 3:24, 25), but it is misleading to conclude from this that personal qualities of Christ's actual obedience are being directly or immediately imparted (given) or infused (poured in) to the believer without faith that freely becomes active in love. The faith that saves is faith that trusts in Christ so as to work in love (Calvin, Inst. 3.16-18).

2. Sin Made Apparent by the Law

The law reveals sin, makes our sin more clear to us. "[Paul] says that sins were made apparent by the law, not abolished. He says not that there was no sin but only that it was not counted. Once the law was given, sin was not taken away, but it began to be counted" (Augustine on Romans 27-28, 9).[23]

"So far was the law from being the cure for sin that Paul even says that there would not have been sin at all had there been no law! By 'law' Paul means the discernment which comes by both the natural law and the law of Moses. For without this discernment, nobody would be able to call sin by its name, since there would be no way of knowing the difference between good and evil" (Theodore of Mopsuestia, Pauline Commentary from the Greek Church).[24]

"How is it then that sin was not imputed, when there was no law? Was it all right to sin, if the law was absent? There had always been a natural law, and it was not unknown, but at that time it was thought to be the only law, and it did not make men guilty before God. For it was not then known that God would judge the human race, and for that reason sin was not imputed, almost as if it did not exist in God's sight and God did not care about it. But when the law was given through Moses, it became clear

22. ACW 31:135-39.
23. ACCS NT 6:139.
24. NTA 15:118; ACCS NT 6:139.

that God did care about human affairs and that in the future wrongdoers would not escape without punishment" (Ambrosiaster, Commentary on Paul's Epistles).[25]

"Sin was in the world before the law of Moses came, and it was counted, though not according to that law. Rather, it was counted according to the law of nature, by which we have learned to distinguish good and evil" (Diodore of Tarsus, Pauline Commentary from the Greek Church).[26]

Paul made it clear that "no one is justified by works of the law" (Gal. 2:16). Jerome explained: "Consider how many are the precepts of the law which no one can fulfill. And it must also be said that some works of the law are done even by those who do not know it. But those who perform it are not justified, because this happens without faith in Christ" (Epistle to the Galatians 1.2.16).[27]

3. Works Righteousness Rejected

Paul reproved those "who because of their self-confidence rejected grace and as a result did not believe in Christ. The Jews, he says, seek to establish a righteousness of their own that comes from the law, not that the law was established by them but rather that they had placed their righteousness in the law which comes from God by supposing that they were able to fulfill this law by themselves. For they were ignorant of the righteousness of God, not that righteousness whereby God is righteous [according to the divine nature], but the one which comes to man from God [according to grace]" (Augustine, Grace and Free Will 12.24).[28]

Paul writes: "For, being ignorant of the righteousness that comes from God, and seeking to establish their own, they did not submit to God's righteousness" (Rom. 10:3). An anonymous Latin writer comments: "By 'their own righteousness' Paul means the law of the Pharisees. For the sacrifices of the law and the other things which were a shadow of the truth, which were to be fulfilled in Christ, ceased to operate once he had come. But this they did not want to believe. The apostle was right to talk of their

---

25. CSEL 81:167, 169; ACCS NT 6:139.
26. NTA 15:83; ACCS NT 6:139.
27. PL 26:344A-B (413); ACCS NT 8:30-31.
28. FC 59:277; ACCS NT 6:272.

own righteousness, because it was not of God, but of themselves" (Anonymous, The Holy Letter of St. Paul to the Romans).[29]

All works whatever are expressly excluded from any interest in our justification before God. What works are excluded? Not only those of the ceremonial law, but also all works pretending righteousness of their own. All works done in the strength of our own wills before believing are excluded from justification.

"A Gentile can be sure that he is justified by faith without doing the works of the law (Rom. 3:28), e.g., circumcision or new moons or the veneration of the sabbath," according to Ambrosiaster (Commentary on Paul's Epistles).[30] But justification "must not be understood in such a way as to say that a man who has received faith and continues to live is righteous, even though he leads a wicked life," wrote Augustine (Questions 76.1).[31]

The principle of justification by faith alone immediately removes any distinction between Jews and Gentiles, since everyone must come to Christ in the same way — by faith. Origen pungently quipped: "Here Paul gives a short sharp answer to those who would say that there is one God for the Jews and another for the Gentiles, i.e., one God of the law and another of the gospel" (Commentary on the Epistle to the Romans 2:140).[32] Paul bluntly asked: "Is God the God of Jews only? Is he not the God of Gentiles also? Yes, of Gentiles also" (Rom. 3:29). "One righteous person," according to Clement of Alexandria, "is no different from another righteous person, whether Jew or Greek" (Stromata 6.6).[33]

Ambrosiaster, commenting on Romans 3:29, offered two biblical examples: "Some Gentiles actually went with the Israelites into the desert of Egypt, and the Israelites were ordered to accept them as long as they agreed to be circumcised and eat unleavened bread, or the Passover, together with the rest of them (Exod. 12:48ff.). Then again Cornelius, a Gentile who was not judaized, received the gift of God, and it is clear from Holy Scripture that he was justified (cf. Acts 10:31)" (Commentary on Paul's Epistles).[34]

29. ENPK 2:71-72; ACCS NT 6:272.
30. CSEL 81 ad loc.; ACCS NT 6:104.
31. FC 70:195; ACCS NT 6:105.
32. ACCS NT 6:105.
33. ANF 2:491; ACCS NT 6:105.
34. CSEL 81 ad loc.; ACCS NT 6:105-6.

"If God is God of all," Chrysostom added, in reference to Gentiles, "then he takes care of all, and if he takes care of all, then he saves all alike by faith" (Homilies on Romans 7),[35] that is, insofar as they trust in God's righteousness.

4. Is the Law Overthrown?

"Do we then overthrow the Law by this faith? By no means!" (Rom. 3:31a). Justification by faith in Christ fulfills what the Law was trying to demonstrate, but which it could not achieve by itself. "Paul says that the law is not nullified by faith but fulfilled. For its status is confirmed when faith bears witness that what it said would come has actually happened. . . . Paul does not nullify the law when he says that it must come to an end, because he asserts that at the time it was given it was rightly given, but now it does not have to be kept any longer. In the law itself it is said that a time would come when the promise would be fulfilled and the law would no longer have to be kept. . . . 'Behold the days are coming, says the Lord, when I will make a new covenant with the house of Israel and the house of Judah, not like the covenant which I made with their fathers'" (Jer. 31:31-32; Ambrosiaster, Commentary on Paul's Epistles).[36]

Origen adds: "Whoever does not believe in Christ, of whom Moses wrote in the law, destroys the law. But whoever believes in Christ, of whom Moses wrote, confirms the law through faith. . . . The Lord himself said: 'I have not come to abolish the law, but to fulfill it' (Matt. 5:17). None of the saints nor even the Lord himself has destroyed the law. Rather its glory, which is temporal and transient, has been destroyed and replaced by a glory which is eternal and permanent" (Commentary on the Epistle to the Romans 2:148, 152).[37]

"On the contrary, we uphold the Law" (Rom. 3:31b). "Paul's use of the word *uphold* shows that the law was failing," wrote Chrysostom. "The purpose of the law was to make man righteous, but it had no power to do that. But when faith came it achieved what the law could not do, for once a man believes he is immediately justified. Faith therefore established what

35. NPNF 1 11:379; ACCS NT 6:106.
36. CSEL 81 ad loc.; ACCS NT 6:107.
37. ACCS NT 6:107.

the law intended and brought to fulfillment what its provisions aimed for. Consequently faith has not abolished the law but perfected it" (Homilies on Romans 7).[38]

"The law was a shadow," noted Cyril of Alexandria, "but even so it presented an image of the truth. Furthermore, the truth hardly destroys its images; rather it makes them clearer" (Commentary on Romans).[39]

"How should the law be upheld," reflected Augustine, "if not by righteousness? By a righteousness, moreover, which is of faith, for what could not be fulfilled through the law is fulfilled through faith" (Augustine, On Romans 19, 7).[40]

5. Neither Circumcision Nor Uncircumcision Yields Advantage

"Since God is one, he will justify the circumcised on the ground of their faith and the uncircumcised through their faith" (Rom. 3:30b). "Neither the circumcision nor the uncircumcision enjoys any advantage in this," noted Origen (Commentary on the Epistle to the Romans 2:142).[41] "By 'the circumcised,'" commented Ambrosiaster, "Paul means the Jews who have been justified by their faith in the promise and who believe that Jesus is the Christ whom God had promised in the law. By 'the uncircumcised' he means the Gentiles who have been justified with God by their faith in Christ. Thus God has justified both Jews and Gentiles. For because God is one, everyone has been justified in the same way. What benefit then is there in circumcision? Or what disadvantage is there in uncircumcision when only faith produces worthiness and merit?" (Commentary on Paul's Epistles).[42]

"There is only one God, who is Lord of all, both Jew and Gentile," argued Chrysostom. "Even in ancient times the blessings of providence were shared by both, although in different ways. The Jews had the written law, and the Gentiles had the natural law, but in this they lacked nothing, because if they tried hard enough, they could always surpass the Jews in their observance. . . . If there was no difference then, much less is there any now,

38. NPNF 1 11:380; ACCS NT 6:107.
39. PG 74 ad loc.; ACCS NT 6:108.
40. ACCS NT 6:107.
41. ACCS NT 6:106.
42. CSEL 81 ad loc.; ACCS NT 6:106.

and this Paul establishes even more firmly by demonstrating that both alike stand in equal need of faith" (Homilies on Romans 7).[43]

The turning point at which Paul parted ways with the Pharisaic Judaism of his day was his recognition of the grace that allowed him to trust in Christ alone for righteousness. What amazed him was stubborn resistance to receiving this good news. The choice to be made is whether we will cling to our own righteousness, or that of Christ's.

6. Counting All Loss for Christ

"If any man thinks he has reason for confidence in the flesh, I have more. Circumcised the eighth day, of the people of Israel, of the tribe of Benjamin" (Phil. 3:4, 5a). "I do not come from a family that was only partially Jewish. I am a plant of freedom, a son of Rachel the beloved, on whose behalf the patriarch himself endured slavery" (Theodoret, Epistle to the Philippians 3.5).[44]

Paul described himself as "a Hebrew born of Hebrews; as touching the law a Pharisee, as to zeal a persecutor of the church" (Phil. 3:5-6). "'When I was harrying the church,' [Paul] says, 'I was not driven by love of honor or vainglory or jealousy, like the rulers of the Jews. I was burning with zeal for the law'" (Theodoret, Epistle to the Philippians 3.6).[45]

"As to righteousness under the law blameless. But whatever gain I had I counted as loss for the sake of Christ" (Phil. 3:6-7).

We are to give thanks for the law, and not despise it. "The false teachers say about this passage: 'See, the law is a *loss*, it is *refuse*. How then do you say it is of God?' . . . He does not say 'the law is privation,' but 'I count it loss.' And when he spoke of gain, he did not say, 'I count it,' but *it was*. For the latter was true by nature, the former in his own estimation. So, whatever gain I had in the law, I count as loss 'on account of Christ.' How then was the law ever *a gain*, and not in supposition but in fact? Consider what a great thing it was to restore the human form to people who had been turned to beasts. And without the law, there would be no grace. How so? Because the law served as a bridge. It was not possible to be raised from this extreme lowliness. So the law served as a ladder. Note that when a per-

---

43. NPNF 1 11:379; ACCS NT 6:106.
44. CPE 2:59; ACCS NT 8:269.
45. CPE 2:59-60; ACCS NT 8:269.

son has gone up a ladder, he no longer needs it. Yet he does not despise it but gives it thanks, because it is due to the ladder that he is in the state of no longer needing it. . . . It is not the law that is a privation but apostasy from Christ through adherence to the law. So when it leads us away from Christ it is a loss. When it leads us to him, no longer so" (Chrysostom, Hom. on Philippians 12.3.7-9).[46]

"Indeed I count everything as loss because of the surpassing worth of knowing Christ Jesus my Lord. For his sake I have suffered the loss of all things, and count them as refuse in order that I may gain Christ" (Phil. 3:8). Theodoret argues that "'refuse' means the denser and harder part of the chaff. It carries the grain but is discarded once the grain has been collected" (Epistle to the Philippians 3.8).[47] The same refuse metaphor used by Abraham, Job, and David was picked up by Paul: "He had read that Abraham, when he confessed himself to be refuse and ashes, found God's grace in his extreme humility (Gen. 18:27). He had read that Job, sitting on his refuse heap, had recovered all his losses (Job 2:8; 42:10ff.). He had read in David's prophecy that 'God raises the needy from the earth and the pauper from the refuse'" (Ps. 113:7; Ambrose, On Penitence 2.1.4).[48]

The Christian's righteousness is not his own, based on law. "Now what does [Paul] mean, 'not having my own righteousness' (Phil. 3:9a), when that law was not his but God's? He can only have called it his own righteousness because, although it was from the law, he used to think that he could fulfill it without the aid of the grace that is through Christ" (Augustine, On Grace and Free Will 26).[49]

"But that which is through faith in Christ, the righteousness from God that depends on faith" (Phil. 3:9b). "Righteousness comes from faith, which means that it too is a gift of God. For since this righteousness belongs to God, it is an unmerited gift. And the gifts of God greatly exceed any achievements of our own zeal" (Chrysostom, Hom. on Philippians 12.3.7-9).[50]

---

46. IOEP 5:123; ACCS NT 8:269-70.
47. CPE 2:60; ACCS NT 8:270.
48. CSEL 73:164; ACCS NT 8:270.
49. PL 44:896; ACCS NT 8:270.
50. IOEP 5:125; ACCS NT 8:270.

7. The Power of His Resurrection

The power of his resurrection is known through faith. "Knowledge therefore comes through faith, and without faith there is no knowledge. How so? It is only through faith that we know the power of his resurrection. For what reasoning could demonstrate the resurrection to us? None, but it is through faith. And if the resurrection of Christ in the flesh is known through faith, how can the nativity of the Word be comprehended by reason?" (Chrysostom, Hom. on Philippians 12.3.10-11).[51]

Paul prayed that "if possible I may attain the resurrection from the dead" (Phil. 3:11), by sharing in his suffering. "We who believe in Christ endure sufferings with him and indeed all sufferings, even as far as the cross and death. From the knowledge of all these and from the sharing in suffering comes resurrection. And thus, as we are sharers in his death and his burden, we are enabled to share his resurrection" (Marius Victorinus, Epistle to the Philippians 3.10-11).[52]

"Not only sufficient but superabundant indeed is the righteousness that comes from faith. This salvation is freely given by the grace of God through the knowledge of Christ. It can hardly be said to be a gift of the law. For to know rightly the mystery of his incarnation and passion and resurrection is the perfection of life and the treasure of wisdom" (Theodoret, Epistle to the Philippians 3.9-10).[53]

Gregory of Nazianzus, in his Oration on Holy Baptism (Theological Orations 40, sec. 45),[54] beautifully gathers together all these themes: "There is no stain where God is and from whom salvation comes. On behalf of the whole of suffering humanity, the one who is wholly man and wholly God comes, that he might bestow salvation on the whole of it, taking away the whole of sin's condemnation; in his Godhead not subject to suffering, but suffering in the humanity he assumed; made man as much for your sake as you are made holy for his. He was led to death on behalf of the lawless, crucified and buried so as to taste of death; who rose again on the third day, and ascended into heaven so that he might take you with him

---

51. IOEP 5:126; ACCS NT 8:271.
52. BT 1972:102 (1220B); ACCS NT 8:271.
53. CPE 2:60-61; ACCS NT 8:271.
54. FEF 2:37-8*; cf. NPNF 2 7:377.

who were prostrate; who will come again in his glorious parousia, to judge the living and the dead."

The evidence has shown that there is a stable, explicit, consensual tradition of exegesis of Paul's teaching of justification firmly established a thousand years before Luther. Now we turn to the definition of grace.

PART TWO

GRACE ALONE

CHAPTER ONE

Why Imputed Grace
Dislodges All Boasting

Grace is the divine good will offered to those who do not deserve it and can never earn it.

A. Defining Grace

Grace is the favor shown by God to sinners. Grace is a pivotal word in all biblical and classic Christian teaching. It embraces all the blessings of salvation. It encompasses all the gifts by which God communicates his own self-giving.

As the unmerited favor of God, grace may point to:

- an era of history in which God's mercy is shown to transcend the law; or
- an encompassing relation of reconciliation of humanity with God; or
- a special gift that enables one to perform a distinctive service by God's help.

1. Scriptural Terms for God's Unmerited Mercy

Grace is a divine attribute revealing the heart of God. The disposition of God is most clearly revealed as unmerited good will, unearned favor even toward the ungodly (Rom. 5:15-21). This disposition is expressed and communicated in the church's ministry of Word and Table whose care of souls offers grace to all.

By grace the sovereign God freely moves toward sinners to offer reconciling forgiveness, a new birth of freedom, and adoption into the family of God.

The Greek word for grace is χάρις (variously nuanced as graciousness, free giving, favor, help, benefaction, an act of good will, a sign of favor, that which causes or accompanies joy, or a quality in God actualized on the cross). Grace is the basis of justification and is also manifested in it. It comes from χαρίζομαι, to give, to favor or gladden, to forgive, hearten, and enliven by showing clemency and mercy. Our words charisma and charismatic derive from χάρις. The Latin parallel is *gratia*, which is the root of the English word for grace.

Χάρις is intrinsically and by definition a gift (χάρισμα). Hence it can never be rightly regarded as a human achievement. The plural, χαρίσματα, points to the many gifts of the Spirit. They are freely offered amid present human circumstances, daily events, and historical limitations. God uses ordinary means to communicate extraordinary blessings and benefits. Χάρις points to a divine disposition to grant goodness and mercy readily, freely, abundantly.

The divine disposition to work in us is grace. The blessings that ensue from the unmerited favor of God are also called grace. Grace may be a gift given, a favor received, or a privilege granted.

These gifts are always received only by means of faith. When something comes as a "Godsend," faith knows that God is sending it to us freely as a gift.

The Hebrew words that attest this unmerited divine disposition are *chen* (gracious, *channun*), and *chesed* (mercy, steadfast love). The God of Israel is gracious and merciful (2 Chron. 30:9; Neh. 9:17), slow to anger, full of compassion, and gracious (Ps. 86:15; 111:4; 112:2).

Grace is offered when good will is shown freely and out of pure benevolence, especially by one who is not obliged to show it.

The underlying motive of God's saving action is simply stated: "He saved us, not because of righteous things we had done, but because of his mercy" (Titus 3:5).

2. The Wooing of Sinners

The engaging and comely act of wooing and giving gifts is an intrinsic aspect of the demeanor of grace. God the Spirit actively seeks out the beloved and offers gifts.

God woos humanity with the most comely means: the beauty of creation, the gifts of covenant sexuality, the restorative power of friendships. When the gifts of men and women dispose them toward behaviors that are admirable, gratifying, beautiful, or desirable, they are rightly called gracious.

God wills to work in God's own way in our hearts, through our choices and actions, amid our families, nations, and social processes. It is by grace that God's self-giving love for humanity is communicated (Rom. 3:24; 6:1; Eph. 1:7; 2:5-8).

B. The Nurture of Gracious Ability

1. The Demeanor of Grace

We call people "gracious" when their personal gifts make their behavior beautiful or desirable.

The Spirit actively seeks out the beloved and offers gifts. This is why grace has rightly come to be associated with attractive and winsome aesthetic qualities. To receive a blow with grace is to do so with wit, good temper, charm, and style. To hit a ball like Sammy Sosa or dance like Cyd Charisse is to do so gracefully, not clumsily, ineptly, awkwardly. To fumble a ball or dance ungracefully is to do so clumsily, ineptly, awkwardly.

Even the cross is made beautiful by grace. When one says "grace before meals," the one who is receiving splendid gifts feels "graced" or blessed and hence "grateful" (Thomas Aquinas, ST I-II, Q110.1).

2. God's Own Gift of Himself

So intimately tied are the terms "grace" and "Spirit" that they flow together as if virtually interchangeable (Acts 6:5, 8). God's Spirit is called "the Spirit of grace" (Heb. 10:29) since it is through the Spirit that the Father confers the grace of the Son upon the celebrating community. From the fullness of this saving event we continue to receive grace upon grace in a persevering series of divine gifts to humanity (John 1:16, 17).

Grace flows from the Father's good will, as it has become mediated to us through the active life and obedient death of the Son. His mission is completed and made effective in our hearts by the work of the Holy Spirit who proceeds from the Father, who comes to convict, convert, regenerate, justify, transform, sanctify, and bring to complete fruition the mission of the Son (Calvin, Inst., 2.2-3).[1]

The grace of God is closely associated with God's love, which engenders a loving spirit in us (Augustine, On the Gift of Perseverance, 14-19).[2] Such a relation seems embedded in the Pauline thought that "The *grace* of our Lord was poured out on me abundantly, *along with the faith and love* that are in Christ Jesus" (1 Tim. 1:14, italics added).[3]

3. The Gift

The Gift is given with the precise intent of being fully and freely received. God by self-giving intends to transform our human habits and behavioral responses. Human responsiveness is called for at every step (Prosper of Aquitaine, Grace and Free Will, 4ff.).[4] The Spirit is sent precisely to nurture faith, hope, love, and the fruits of the Spirit, so that persons can grow through prayer and praise to be as fully reflective as possible of the incomparable goodness of God. Later Catholics and Lutherans would formally agree that the unity of "faith, hope, and love is always dependent on God's unfathomable grace and contributes nothing to justification, about which one could boast before God" (JD 4.3.27).

The triune premise helps the believer to behold the unity of the grace of God, that the grace of God the Father is the grace of God the Son, and the grace of the Son is the grace of God the Spirit, not three graces but the unifying grace of the one God — uncreated, begotten, and proceeding. Ambrosiaster wrote: "Grace and the gift cannot be divided according to the persons of the Father, Son and Holy Spirit but must be understood as

---

1. Barth, CD IV/1, pp. 143ff.
2. NPNF 1 5:530-31.
3. Cf. Thomas Aquinas, ST, I-II, Q110.3-4.
4. FC 7:352ff.

constituting the one work of the undivided unity and nature of the Three" (Commentary on Paul's Epistles).[5]

The grace of the Father is for all creatures, enabling all life, and prior to all choice and all sin. The grace of the Son is particularly given for sinners (Rom. 5:8). The grace of the Spirit administers the finished work of the Son (Novatian, The Trinity 16).[6] While all grace as such is the work of the one triune God, the enabling and appropriation of grace is primarily the constant work of God the Spirit (Ambrose, On the Holy Spirit, I.12).[7]

4. Life as Unearned Gift

Life can only be received. Life is offered as sheer gift. In new birth from above, there is no way for those already dead in their sins even to ask for new life, which being dead in sin they cannot even conceive (Rom. 8:10, 11; Eph. 2:1-5). Apart from grace one cannot even pray for or hope for a re-born relationship to God. No one can simply grasp, claim, or seize the new birth of faith, hope, and love. They are gifts of the Spirit which until given, the unawakened sinner cannot manipulate into conception, birth, or growth. Like Incarnation and Resurrection, the new birth comes on God's own initiative.

God's own Spirit remains sovereignly free, coming and going, working when and where God pleases. The Christian life comes to us on God's own initiative, not our own. We can choose by God's grace to put ourselves in those places and times where God promises to be present. We can avail ourselves of the means of grace, but not so as to control them. They remain precisely grace — sheer gift. The teaching of grace stands as a penetrating challenge to all pretensions of self-sufficiency (Augustine, On Nature and Grace).[8]

5. CSEL 81:133; ACCS NT 7:120-21.
6. ANF 5:625-26.
7. NPNF 2 10:110; Calvin, Inst. 2.2.
8. NPNF 1 5:121ff.

5. Works and Grace Contrasted

The way of grace is sharply contrasted with the way of works, by which we are prone to seek to achieve merit: "And if by grace, then it is no longer by works; if it were, grace would no longer be grace" (Rom. 11:6). "It is clear that because grace is the gift of God there is no reward due for works, but it is granted freely because of the free mercy which intervenes" (Gal. 2:15-16; Ambrosiaster, Commentary on Paul's Epistles).[9]

These ways are contrasted: "Grace shows the love for mankind of the one who gives it, but works demand compensation according to what they are worth" (Diodore of Tarsus, Pauline Commentary from the Greek Church).[10]

Paul compares the first Adam with the second Adam (Christ), and those that derive from them. The apostle employs a series of polarities in Romans 5:12-21 to describe the human condition as:

fallen	being raised up
indebted	solvency
guilty	uprighting
bound	freedom
sold	being bought
disobedient	the obedience of Christ
under judgment unto death	justification unto life

The deep motive of God's saving action is simply stated: "He saved us, not because of righteous things we had done, but because of his mercy" (Titus 3:5). It is simply because God "is rich in mercy" that the faithful have been made "alive with Christ even when we were dead in transgressions — it is by grace you have been saved" (Eph. 2:4, 5).

Readers of scripture find God's grace appearing abundantly with extremely variable flexibility and numerous correlated levels of meaning. As the unmerited favor of God, grace is

- an era of history
- a relation of reconciliation of humanity with God
- a gift enabling one to perform a service.

9. CSEL 81:365; ACCS NT 6:286.
10. NTA 15:102; ACCS NT 6:286.

C. How Grace Grounds Justification:
By Free Grace We Have Full Satisfaction

1. We Are Justified as a Gift

By grace our debt is fully discharged and God's demand for justice satisfied. "Christ, by His obedience and death, did fully discharge the debt of all those that are thus justified, and did make a proper, real and full satisfaction to His Father's justice in their behalf. Yet, in as much as He was given by the Father for them; and His obedience and satisfaction accepted in their stead; and both, freely, not for any thing in them; their justification is only of free grace; that both the exact justice, and rich grace of God might be glorified in the justification of sinners" (Westminster Confession, 11.3).

2. Four Related Metaphorical Arenas:
Forgiving, Pardoning, Accounting, and Reconciling

Four related metaphors flow together in the biblical teaching of justification:

- the offender is forgiven
- the accused is pardoned
- the offense is remitted
- the lost child is welcomed home

In these four arenas of analogy, God's justifying grace shows forth a spectacular cohesion of unified divine gifts. The pivotal turning from repentance to faith is symbolized in four ways as:

an act of forgiveness that encourages
an acquittal that frees from condemnation
a new mode of crediting moral accounts that crosses out the penalty
a divine-human reconciliation and restoration to favor that embraces the wayward child

The scriptural metaphors are more mixed and interactive than this simplified sequence, but their variables are encompassed and summarized by it. Though distinguishable, forgiveness and pardon must be considered conjointly.

3. Forgiving and Pardoning: Are They Distinguishable?

The first of many blessings of saving faith is the forgiveness of sins. This necessarily precedes the reception of all subsequent benefits of the new life. It remains an article of the Apostles' Creed to confess: "I believe in the forgiveness of sins."

Forgiveness and pardon are related metaphors belonging to very different arenas of analogy:

- Pardoning is an action that takes place in a courtroom.
- Forgiving is an act that occurs within primary face-to-face relationships, especially in the family and sustained friendships.

The judge may have the authority to pardon while lacking the authority to divinely forgive. The loving parent can personally forgive, but such forgiveness might be presumptuous or unfitting in relation to the rigor of the law in a courtroom. Though distinguishable, they are complementary, and often intermingle in the New Testament narratives. It is through divine forgiveness that a judicial acquittal of pardon is offered by the final Judge.

It is not the case that those free from condemnation are then forgiven. That would reverse the order. Rather, those forgiven are thereby freed from condemnation (John 3:16; Rom. 4:5; 5:1, 16; Gal. 2:16).

These are different ways of looking at the same event: The sinner is being forgiven through the mercy of God in Christ, which enables the sinner to be declared by God the judge as justified, since the sinner is united with Christ's righteousness, so that one's sins are covered over. Each verb amplifies the meaning of the other: God gives, forgives, justifies, pardons, remits, covers sin, and reckons faith for righteousness. These are not different events, but differing language for the same event. One is declared justified because of the pardon.

4. Distinguishing Pardon and Justification

It is divine mercy that pardons. It is divine justice that justifies. To *pardon* is to waive the execution of the penalties of the law. To *justify* is to declare that the demands of the law are truly and justly satisfied, not ignored or waived.

When a pardon is granted to one who is guilty, it is not strictly speaking according to the law, but in a way that transcends the law through grace. Grace mercifully covers the demands of the law without ceasing to be just.

Only mercy and justice together with a single voice can justify. Justification is that key moment in the history of salvation in which the righteousness of God is declared in relation to the history of sin, yet without offence to the justice of God. One who is justified is declared just on the basis of the pardon through which guilt is mercifully and justly remitted.

5. Only God Can Justly Forgive Sin

In Christ, pardon and justification intermingle almost indistinguishably, so that one whom God pardons is justified and one whom God justifies is pardoned. Even if not strictly equivalent, they are inseparable. Where one is mentioned in scripture, the other is implied (Mark 1:4; Luke 1:77; 3:3; Acts 2:38; 5:31; 10:43; Eph. 1:7; Rom. 3:24; Titus 3:7). For this reason pardon and justification at times appear in scripture as virtually synonymous terms: "Therefore, my brothers, I want you to know that through Jesus the forgiveness of sins is proclaimed to you. Through him everyone who believes is justified from everything you could not be justified from by the law of Moses" (Acts 13:38, 39; cf. Luke 18:13, 14; Rom. 4:5, 8).

Only the crucified Lord could at the same time remain "just" and "forgive us our sins" (1 John 1:9; Rom. 3:26). Only one who is truly human and truly God could justly pardon without demeaning divine justice.

Thus grace reigns through merciful righteousness, but not by mercy alone as if separable from justice. Forgiveness is consistent with God's righteous character only in the light of the cross: "If we confess our sins, he is faithful and just and will forgive us our sins and purify us from all unrighteousness" (1 John 1:9).

6. Who Can Pardon?

No one can move from conviction to pardon simply by examining one's own conscience or by the force of will or by limited human reasoning. Pardon is exclusively an act of grace offered and revealed by the incomparably holy and merciful One who pardons.

My own word of pardon to myself is always finally self-contrived, hence insufficient, artificial, shallow, and ungrounded. Pardon must be based upon the valid pardoning agent. This can only be the eternal One who is infinitely just, holy, and merciful. Only this One is full of grace without ceasing to be full of truth. It is finally by Another that one is forgiven, not simply by a human voice, but by One authorized to forgive sin: God alone (Ps. 25:11; Isa. 40:1, 2). One may despairingly will oneself to be pardoned, but without the actual, eventful pardon of God, that willing remains in despair.

Reason can analyze the need for pardon, as in psychoanalysis, but reason as such cannot pardon. Through reason one may learn that God is just, but it is hardly a reasonable deduction that God would justify sinners precisely while they were yet ungodly (Rom. 5:8).

Conscience is the last and least likely of all human faculties to pardon sin. Its main constructive function in the presence of sin is to accuse. "If you, O Lord, kept a record of sins, O Lord, who could stand? But with you there is forgiveness" (Ps. 130:3, 4).

When his detractors asked Jesus: "Who can forgive sins but God alone?" (Luke 5:21), they were asking a profound question, yet they did not recognize that it was only the incarnate God standing in their midst who was able to announce pardon to the paralytic, which he did: "Friend, your sins are forgiven" (Luke 5:20).

7. Forgiveness as Given

Forgiveness can occur only when freely given away. The Anglo-Saxon root is *for-*, away, and *giefan*, to give, corresponding with the Greek ἄφεσις, a letting go. Anyone who forgives another for being wronged is engaging in a gracious act that shares in God's own grace.

Justification is a gift of God to which the human recipient has no intrinsic right or claim — except by trusting in the righteousness of the Giver (Eph. 1:6, 7; 2:7, 8; Rom. 4:4; John 3:16; Titus 2:11).

If it were merited, forgiveness could be claimed as something due, which would subvert the need for forgiveness. The primary premise of forgiveness is lack of merit, not merit (Second Council of Orange).[11] Insofar as divine forgiveness is considered a matter of our merit, there is no need to forgive.

Forgiveness is a costly gift, since the one forgiving cancels the debt. The cost is the death of the Lord of glory. What is due is forfeited. Someone takes responsibility for another's liability or debt. The distinguishing element of for*give*ness is that it is precisely a gift.

God's forgiveness of our sins involves and requires God's taking our sins upon himself, bearing them on the cross. He accepts the penalty for us. He is punished where the sinner justly should have been punished under law.

Wherever forgiveness characterizes and sustains a relationship, it is no longer dominated by charges, counterclaims, jealousy, or attempts to recover damages, but by overflowing love, reconciliation, and grace. Love covers a multitude of sins (James 5:20). In forgiving, one graciously gives up nursing resentment, as well as all debts and leverage against another.

The Lord's Prayer makes it clear that anyone who receives God's forgiveness is called to share it with others. The prayer makes these two dimensions inseparable: God is forgiving us; we are forgiving others (Luke 11:4). Jesus held the connection rigorously — "if you do not forgive men their sins, your Father will not forgive your sins" (Matt. 6:15).

D. Imputed Righteousness

If one "does a piece of work, his wages are not 'counted' as a favor; they are paid as debt. But if without any work to his credit he simply puts his faith in him who acquits the guilty, then his faith is indeed 'counted as righteousness'" (Rom. 4:4, 5 NEB).

---

11. SCD 176ff., pp. 75ff.

1. The Bookkeeping Analogy

The New Testament makes frequent use of the bookkeeping analogy: imputing or crediting something to another's account. To impute (λογίζομαι) is to account debt or credit to one person as coming from another.

Here the metaphorical arena shifts from the court to the accounting office. What happened in the courtroom has to be registered in the court records.

This is what is meant by imputation: One's debit balance may be charged to another. Or someone's plus balance may be credited to another. By imputation a debit or credit is applied to one's own account due to an action of another. Guilt or righteousness may thereby be attributed to one on account of the offense or merit of another. Indebtedness may be made into a credit balance if the creditor chooses to cancel the debt.

The analogy of imputation is embedded decisively in all biblical teaching of justifying grace. This is seen in Paul's crucial phrase: "faith is credited [λογίζεται] as righteousness" (Rom. 4:5). My sins are charged to Christ! Christ's obedience is offered for my account. Although Wesley did not want the language of imputation to lead to human unresponsiveness, he did confirm the right biblical use of the language of imputation: "Faith may be said to be imputed to us for righteousness, as it is the sole condition of our acceptance" (Wesley, NUNT, Rom. 4:9).[12] Our sin has been reckoned or accounted to Christ, so that Christ paid the penalty for our sin, becoming a curse for us. Sin is mercifully being not counted against or imputed to the sinner who trusts Christ (Rom. 4:22-24; 2 Cor. 5:19; Calvin, Inst. 3.11-15).

2. Discharging Sin and Crediting Righteousness

Justification means both the discharging of the debt of sin, and the crediting (imputation) of Christ's righteousness (Clement of Alexandria, Stromata, V.5).[13]

Debt is discharged while substitutionary payment is credited. This is the biblical metaphorical ground of the substitutionary view of the atoning work of God on the cross.

12. WNB, p. 499.
13. ANF II:444-46; cf. Calvin, Inst., 4.16-17.

Both directions of this reversal are quite explicit in Paul:

- Sin is not charged against the believing sinner — for "God was reconciling the world to himself in Christ, *not counting* men's sins against them" (2 Cor. 5:19, italics added); and
- Christ's righteousness is accredited to the believing sinner, who is "found in him, not having a righteousness of my own that comes from the law, but that which is through faith in Christ — the *righteousness that comes from God and is by faith*" (Phil. 3:9, italics added).
- Righteousness is thus reckoned to one *who does not work but trusts God,* whose *faith is credited as righteousness* (Rom. 4:5).

In this way imputed righteousness implies two forms of re-crediting:

- imputation of the sins of the penitent faithful to Christ, and
- imputation of Christ's righteousness to the penitent faithful.

A correlated metaphor: Christ has taken the church for his bride. Thus the merits of the righteous groom cover over all the inadequacies of the sinful bride. Our sin is imputed to Christ, his righteousness is imputed to us.

3. The New Accounting

The accounting metaphor accords believers the standing of uprightness which they do not reach by their own willing or acting. The believer is dealt with in debt-accounting as if he actually had a clear account, due to God's gracious intervention. One cannot on one's own achieve an adequate righteousness. God has mercifully provided it.

This is why one's own moral actions and self-justifications are not the basis for gaining any standing whatever in God's presence. Only in the cross is it possible to see that sin is forgiven without offending God's own righteousness.

But how can God remain holy if sin is easily dismissed? That is just the point: it is not an easy dismissal. It required a cross, a death, a burial. The cross is a sacrificial offering that substitutes Christ's goodness for our sin. The burden of our sin is transferred directly from our shoulders to Christ's cross (Rom. 3:21-25; 2 Cor. 5:21).

4. Remission of Debt

A related metaphor comes from commerce, and more specifically slavery. It is *remission*. It was used in the New Testament to explain justifying grace, especially as to its outcome of freedom.

Remission refers to that act by which debt or guilt or penalty is finally and absolutely set aside. It is literally "sent back" (Latin: *remittere*). To remit is to cancel a debt altogether. In this way, "everyone who believes in him receives forgiveness [ἄφεσις] of sins" (Acts 10:43).

The remission picture is especially powerful when applied to the desperate and impotent condition of the slave. Typically there would be no way the slave could ever pay the price to be remitted from his own debt. Someone else has to remit it.

5. Summarizing the Confluence of Biblical Metaphors

The Gospel of Jesus Christ (GJC, 1999) fittingly summarizes this classic teaching for modern evangelicals: "God's justification of those who trust him, according to the Gospel, is a decisive transition, here and now, from a state of condemnation and wrath because of their sins to one of acceptance and favor by virtue of Jesus' flawless obedience culminating in his voluntary sin-bearing death. God 'justifies the wicked' (ungodly: Rom. 4:5) by imputing (reckoning, crediting, counting, accounting) righteousness to them and ceasing to count their sins against them (Rom. 4:1-8). Sinners receive through faith in Christ alone 'the gift of righteousness' (Rom. 1:17, 5:17; Phil. 3:9) and thus become 'the righteousness of God' in him who was 'made sin' for them (2 Cor. 5:21)."[14]

"As our sins were reckoned to Christ, so Christ's righteousness is reckoned to us. This is justification by the imputation of Christ's righteousness. All we bring to the transaction is our need of it. Our faith in the God who bestows it, the Father, the Son, and the Holy Spirit, is itself the

14. GJC, Preamble.

fruit of God's grace. Faith links us savingly to Jesus, but inasmuch as it involves an acknowledgment that we have no merit of our own, it is confessedly not a meritorious work."[15]

"We affirm that the doctrine of the imputation (reckoning or counting) both of our sins to Christ and of his righteousness to us, whereby our sins are fully forgiven and we are fully accepted, is essential to the biblical Gospel (2 Cor. 5:19-21). We deny that we are justified by the righteousness of Christ infused into us or by any righteousness that is thought to inhere within us."[16]

E. The Fathers Teach the Unmerited Grace of the Triune God

1. The Grace of the Triune God

God's Spirit is "the Spirit of grace" (Heb. 10:29; Zech. 12:10). It is through the Spirit that the Father confers the grace of the Son. From the fullness of this saving event we continue to receive grace upon grace in an abiding series of divine gifts to humanity (John 1:16, 17).

Grace flows from the Father's good will, as it has become mediated to us through the active life and obedient death of the Son. His mission is completed and made effective in our hearts by the work of the Holy Spirit. The Spirit comes to convict, convert, regenerate, justify, transform, sanctify, and bring to complete fruition the mission of the Son.

The grace of God is one as Father, Son, and Spirit, and not divided. Triune teaching points to the unity of grace. There are not three separable slices of grace in history but the unifying grace of the one God — uncreated, begotten, and proceeding.

The common grace of the Father enables all life, and is prior to all choice and all sin. The grace of the Son is particularly given for repenting sinners (Rom. 5:8). The grace of the Spirit administers the finished work of the Son. While all grace as such is the work of the triune God, the enabling and appropriation of grace is primarily the constant work of God the Spirit (Ambrose, On the Holy Spirit, I.12).[17]

---

15. GJC, Preamble.
16. GJC, Affirmations and Denials 12.
17. NPNF 2 10:110; Calvin, Inst. 2.2.

"Justification thus means that Christ himself is our righteousness, in which we share through the Holy Spirit in accord with the will of the Father" (JD 15). The unity of the triune God is beheld in God's varied acts of grace. "Here is the intertwining of the Trinity and the unity of power which brings all salvation to fulfillment. The love of God has sent us Jesus the Savior, by whose grace we have been saved. The fellowship of the Holy Spirit makes it possible for us to possess the grace of salvation, for he guards those who are loved by God and saved by the grace of Christ, so that the completeness of the Three may be the saving fulfillment of mankind" (Ambrosiaster, Commentary on Paul's Epistles).[18] The grace of the triune God is undivided. "Where the fellowship is of the Spirit, it is also of the Son, and where the grace is of the Son, it is also of the Father and the Spirit" (Chrysostom, Homilies on the Epistles of Paul to the Corinthians 30.3).[19] It is for this whole diversity and range of triune grace that we pray, with Paul, when he prayed: "The grace of the Lord Jesus Christ and the love of God and the fellowship of the Holy Spirit be with you all" (2 Cor. 13:14).

2. The Spirit Is the Gift

God not only gives himself, but actively *enables* the Gift to be received. The Gift is given with the intent of being fully and freely received. So intimately tied are the terms "grace" and "Spirit" that they flow together as if virtually interchangeable (Acts 6:5, 8). In classic Christianity the Spirit was often called simply the Gift (Thomas Aquinas, ST I-I, Q38).[20]

As "there are different kinds of gifts, but the same Spirit," so "there are different kinds of working, but the same God works all of them in all. Now to each one the manifestation of the Spirit is given for the common good" (1 Cor. 12:4, 6, 7). The Gift-giver and Gift are one (John 14:26; 20:22; Acts 1:16; 11:15; 19:2-6). As the Son is Priest without ceasing to be Sacrifice, the Spirit is Gift without ceasing to be Giver.

Lutherans and Catholics have confessed together that "good works — a Christian life lived in faith, hope, and love — follow justification and

18. CSEL 81:314; ACCS NT 7:315.
19. NPNF 1 12:418-19; ACCS NT 7:316.
20. I:191-93.

are its fruits" (JD 4.7.37). And they confess together that "on the strength of Christ's death and resurrection they can build on the effective promise of God's grace in Word and Sacrament and so be sure of this grace" (JD 4.6.34). "We also confess that God's commandments retain their validity for the justified and that Christ has by his teaching and example expressed God's will, which is a standard for the conduct of the justified also" (JD 4.5.31). "Protestant doctrine understands substantially under the one word 'faith,' what Catholic doctrine (following 1 Cor. 13:13) sums up in the triad of 'faith, hope, and love'" (JD p. 32). These irenic clarifications are bringing divided Christians closer together on the core teaching of grace.

3. The God of All Grace

Grace is great, majestic beyond imagining (Acts 4:33). Grace is sovereign (Rom. 5:21). "[God] is called the God of all grace (1 Pet. 5:10) because he is good and the giver of all good things" (Clement of Alexandria, *Adumbrationes*).[21]

"Every perfect gift comes from the Father of lights" (James 1:17). "James calls God the Father of intelligent lights, that is to say, the illuminator of all rational beings, from whom, as the giver of these things, the divine gifts come to human beings" (Didymus the Blind).[22] "No one deserves to receive anything from the Father of lights, from whom every good gift comes down, except by receiving what he does not deserve" (Augustine, Letters 186).[23]

God is the Giver of grace (Ps. 84:11). God's throne is the throne of grace (Heb. 4:16). The riches of grace are exhibited in God's kindness through Christ (Eph. 2:7). The glory of grace is manifested when we receive the gifts offered by God in Christ (Eph. 1:6). "So that our love for him may become more fervent," says Chrysostom, "he desires nothing from us except our salvation. He does not need our service or anything else but does everything for this end. One who openly expresses praise and wonder at God's grace will be more eager and zealous" (Hom. on Ephesians 1.1.6).[24]

---

21. FGNK 3:82; ACCS NT 11:125.
22. PG 39:1751-52; ACCS NT 11:14.
23. FC 30:199; ACCS NT 11:15.
24. IOEP 4:110; ACCS NT 8:113.

The grace and favor of God was upon Christ (Luke 2:40; John 3:34). Christ spoke with grace (Luke 4:22; cf. Ps. 45:2), and was full of grace (John 1:14). Grace came to us by Christ (John 1:17; Rom. 5:15; 1 Cor. 1:4).

Grace is rich (Eph. 1:7; 2:7). Grace is abundant (2 Cor. 9:14; Rom. 5:15, 17, 20). "God is able to provide you with every blessing in abundance, so that you may always have enough of everything and may provide in abundance for every good work" (2 Cor. 9:8). Grace is all-sufficient (2 Cor. 12:9). Grace is full of glory (Eph. 1:6).

In gracious actions a blessing is bestowed. The active mercy and grace of God, the Life-giver and Helper, have become expressed in time and space through touchable, tastable, visible means. Such acts are freely given, not earned. By these gifts we are blessed (Augustine, Commentary on John, Tractate III.9).[25]

The Macedonian church was a case in point of living out of the abundance of grace, even amid poverty: "For in a severe test of affliction, their abundance of joy and their extreme poverty have overflowed in a wealth of liberality on their part" (2 Cor. 8:2). The faithful found joy even amid a severe test of affliction: "The affliction of the Macedonians did not lead only to sorrow, but also to great rejoicing and generosity. Paul said this in order to prepare the Corinthians to be noble and firm in their sufferings. For they were not merely to be afflicted, they were to use their afflictions as a means of growing in joy" (Chrysostom, Homilies on the Epistles of Paul to the Corinthians 16.2).[26] "For they gave according to their means, as I can testify, and beyond their means, of their own free will" (2 Cor. 8:3). "The greatness of the Macedonians can be seen from the fact that they gave voluntarily, in spite of their poverty" (Chrysostom, Homilies on the Epistles of Paul to the Corinthians 16.3).[27]

F. Receiving Grace, Growing in Grace, Living under Grace

Believers receive grace from Christ (John 1:16). The faithful are what they are by grace (1 Cor. 15:10).

---

25. NPNF 1 7:21.
26. NPNF 1 12:357; ACCS NT 7:270.
27. NPNF 1 12:357; ACCS NT 7:270.

1. Receiving Grace

In receiving grace we give God glory (1 Pet. 5:10, 11). "Grace is the glory of God, not the merit of him who has been freed," according to Prosper of Aquitaine (Grace and Free Will).[28] "It is ultimately the role of the Father and of the Son to proclaim the mystery of faith, because the glory and power belong to them, although they condescend to make use of us and of our preaching."[29]

"Having gifts that differ according to the grace given to us, let us use them" (Rom. 12:6). This occurs "not according to the faith which is from us, but according to the faith which has been given and granted to each person from God" (Anonymous, The Holy Letter of St. Paul to the Romans).[30]

2. Growing in Grace

We are called to grow in grace (Ps. 84:7; Prov. 4:18; Phil. 1:6, 9-11). The faithful grow strong in grace (2 Tim. 2:1; 2 Pet. 3:18).

"And we all, with unveiled face, beholding the glory of the Lord, are being changed into his likeness from one degree of glory to another; for this comes from the Lord who is the Spirit" (2 Cor. 3:18). "We shall all behold him together with uncovered faces. As soon as we are baptized, the soul beams even more brightly than the sun because it is cleansed by the Spirit, and we not only behold God's glory, we receive from it a kind of splendor" (Chrysostom, Homilies on the Epistles of Paul to the Corinthians 7.5).[31]

"God has granted to each of us the special graces needed for the upbuilding of his church, so that we will do what he has indicated should be done, not only without complaint but with joy" (1 Pet. 4:10; Augustine, On Christian Doctrine 1.15).[32]

We are called both to "grow in grace and knowledge" (2 Pet. 3:18). "Grow in the faith which is yours by baptism, and in the knowledge which

28. FC 7:373.
29. Andreas, *Catena*, CEC 82; ACCS NT 11:125.
30. ENPK 2:80; ACCS NT 6:312.
31. NPNF 1 12:313-14; ACCS NT 7:225.
32. FC 2:38; ACCS NT 11:117.

comes from putting that faith into practice" (Hilary of Arles, Introductory Commentary on 2 Peter).[33]

3. Living under Grace

"For sin will have no dominion over you, since you are not under law but under grace" (Rom. 6:14). The faithful live "under grace."

Sin has no dominion. "It is necessary for a person to be under the law as long as he does not receive forgiveness, for by the law's authority sin makes the sinner guilty. Thus the person to whom forgiveness is given and who keeps it by not sinning anymore will neither be ruled by sin nor be under the law. For the authority of the law no longer applies to him; he has been delivered from sin. Those whom the law holds guilty have been turned over to it by sin. Therefore the person who has departed from sin cannot be under the law" (Ambrosiaster, Commentary on Paul's Epistles).[34]

Since you live "under grace," make choices that reflect that reality: "Having shown that they should avoid sinning for the sake of future benefits, Paul goes on to add that they should live as though they were incapable of sinning at all. For if the time was coming when they would be transformed and act as sinless people, then here and now they ought to cleanse their minds of any thought of sin, and earnestly try to do what is good" (Rom. 6:14; Theodore of Mopsuestia, Pauline Commentary from the Greek Church).[35]

What does it mean to live under grace (Rom. 6:14)? "This refers to the third state of man, when in his mind he serves the law of God even though his flesh still serves the law of sin. For he does not obey the desire to sin, even though lusts will continue to court him and urge him to surrender until the body is raised to new life and death is swallowed up in victory. Because we do not give in to evil desires we are under grace, and sin does not reign in our mortal bodies. But the man who is controlled by sin even if he wants to resist it is still under the law and not yet under grace" (Augustine, On Romans 35.13).[36] "Grace causes sin not to have power over

---

33. PL Supp. 3:116; ACCS NT 11:163.
34. CSEL 81:201-3; ACCS NT 6:165-66.
35. NTA 15:122; ACCS NT 6:166.
36. ACCS NT 6:166.

you. Therefore do not trust in yourself, lest sin thereby have much more power over you" (Augustine, Continence 5.12).[37]

Grace ends the reign of sin. "As long as someone is involved in sins he lives according to the old man, but when he is converted into the right way, he is said to be upright. Because it is not impossible for those who have received grace to sin, Paul says: 'Let not sin reign in you.' But he knows well that those who are under grace are strangers to the many and varied commandments of the law, and to their burdens" (Anonymous, The Holy Letter of St. Paul to the Romans).[38]

G. How Protestant Definitions of Grace
Confirm the Patristic Consensus

It is now fitting to compare this classic patristic consensus with the classic Protestant confessions. We look for a Protestant consensus on the meaning of grace. Only then will it become clear that it does not differ substantially from the patristic consensus on grace, since both are thoroughly Pauline.

First, is there in fact a consensual Protestant teaching on justifying grace, the grace that makes possible an upright relation with God? Is there an underlying Protestant doctrine of grace that is shared generally by virtually all Protestants, despite some continuing differences on specific readings of specific scriptures? We believe that there is, and that it can be demonstrated textually by comparison of authoritative texts from these various traditions.

1. Standard Lutheran Confessions

The Augsburg Confession, 1530, Article XVIII states: "Without the grace, help, and activity of the Holy Spirit man is not capable of making himself acceptable to God, of fearing God and believing in God with his whole heart, or of expelling inborn evil lust from his heart. This is accomplished by the Holy Spirit, who is given through the word of God, for Paul says in 1 Cor. 2:14, 'Natural man does not receive the gifts of the Spirit of God.'"[39]

---

37. FC 16:203; ACCS NT 6:166.
38 ENPK 2:42-43; ACCS NT 6:166.
39. CC 74.

Augustine is quoted by the Augsburg Confession on grace in Article XVIII: "These things are said in as many words by Augustine in his Hypognosticon, Book III: 'We grant that all men have a free will, free, inasmuch as it has the judgment of reason; not that it is thereby capable, without God, either to begin, or, at least, to complete anything in things pertaining to God, but only in works of this life, whether good or evil. 'Good' I call those works which spring from the good in nature, such as, willing to labor in the field, to eat and drink, to have a friend, to clothe oneself, to build a house, to marry a wife, to raise cattle, to learn divers useful arts, or whatsoever good pertains to this life. All of these things are not without dependence on the providence of God. Of Him and through Him they are and have their being. 'Evil' I call such works as willing to worship an idol, to commit murder, etc. They [the faithful] condemn the Pelagians and others, who teach that without the Holy Ghost, by the power of nature alone, we are able to love God above all things; also to do the commandments of God as touching 'the substance of the act.' For, although nature is able in a manner to do the outward work (for it is able to keep the hands from theft and murder), yet it cannot produce the inward motions, such as the fear of God, trust in God, chastity, patience, etc."

The Smalcald Articles, XIII declare: "The entire man, both as to his person and his works, is to be called and to be righteous and holy from pure grace and mercy, shed upon us and spread over us in Christ. Therefore we cannot boast of many merits and works, if they are viewed apart from grace and mercy, but as it is written, 1 Corinthians 1:31: 'He that glories, let him glory in the Lord,' namely, that he has a gracious God. For thus all is well. We say, besides, that if good works do not follow, faith is false and not true." Thus the patristic consensual reading of grace according to Paul is reflected in the Lutheran Confessions.

2. Reformed Confessions

Similarly in the Reformed tradition: By grace our debt is fully discharged and God's demand for justice satisfied. "Christ, by His obedience and death, did fully discharge the debt of all those that are thus justified, and did make a proper, real and full satisfaction to his Father's justice in their behalf. Yet, in as much as he was given by the Father for them; and his obedience and satisfaction accepted in their stead; and both, freely, not for any thing in them; their justification is only of free grace; that both the exact justice, and rich grace of God might be glorified in the justification of sinners" (Westminster Confession, 11.3).

Similarly: "Although Christ by his obedience and death, did make a proper, real and full satisfaction to God's justice in the behalf of them that are justified; yet inasmuch as God accepts the satisfaction from a surety [collateral, bond, deposit, guarantee], which he might have demanded of them; and did provide this surety, his only Son, imputing his righteousness to them, and requiring nothing of them for their justification but faith, which also is his gift, their justification is to them of free grace" (Westminster Larger Catechism Q 71).

3. A Congregationalist Standard

Closely tracking Westminster, the Congregationalists' Savoy Declaration confirms the patristic consensus: "Their justification is only of free grace; that both the exact justice, and rich grace of God might be glorified in the justification of sinners."

4. A Baptist Standard

In the Report of the Committee on Baptist Faith and Message (Southern Baptist Convention, 1925): "Article 9: God's Purpose of Grace. Election is the gracious purpose of God, according to which he regenerates, sanctifies and saves sinners. It is perfectly consistent with the free agency of man, and comprehends all the means in connection with the end. It is a most gracious display of God's sovereign goodness, and is infinitely wise, holy, and unchangeable. It excludes boasting and promotes humility. It encourages the use of means in the highest degree."[40] No element here differs from the patristic consensus.

40. CC 347-48.

5. Anglican Standards

Likewise, the Thirty-Nine Articles, X, Of Free Will: "The condition of man after the fall of Adam is such that he cannot turn and prepare himself, by his own natural strength and good works, to faith, and calling upon God. Therefore we have no power to do good works, pleasant and acceptable to God, without the grace of God by Christ preventing [going before] us that we may have a good will, and working with us when we have that good will."[41]

The Irish Articles of Religion, 1615, Of Justification and Faith, Article 35: "Thus the justice and mercy of God do embrace each other: the grace of God not shutting out the justice of God in the matter of our justification, but only shutting out the justice of man (that is to say, the justice of our own works) from being any cause of our deserving our justification."[42]

6. Wesleyan Standards

The Wesleyan amendment to the Thirty-Nine Articles does not change the above Anglican article. The Evangelical United Brethren Confession, which is official teaching of the United Methodist Church, states: "We believe man is fallen from righteousness and, apart from the grace of our Lord Jesus Christ, is destitute of holiness and inclined to evil. Except a man be born again, he cannot see the Kingdom of God. In his own strength, without divine grace, man cannot do good works pleasing and acceptable to God. We believe, however, man influenced and empowered by the Holy Spirit is responsible in freedom to exercise his will for good."[43]

The Wesleyan Church Articles of Religion state: "We have no power to do good works pleasant and acceptable to God without the grace of God by Christ working in us, that we may have a good will, and working with us when we have that good will."[44]

The Nazarene Articles of Faith state: "Through the fall of Adam [man] became depraved so that he cannot now turn and prepare himself

41. DSWT 115.
42. COC 3:432-33.
43. DSWT 141.
44. DSWT 141.

by his own natural strength and works to faith and calling upon God. But we also believe that the grace of God through Jesus Christ is freely bestowed upon all men, enabling all who will to turn from sin to righteousness, believe on Jesus Christ for pardon and cleansing from sin, and follow good works pleasing and acceptable in his sight."[45]

7. Contemporary Evangelicals Speak Together

Contemporary evangelicals spoke with one voice in The Gospel of Jesus Christ (1999) on imputed justifying grace: "We affirm that the righteousness of Christ by which we are justified is properly his own, which he achieved apart from us, in and by his perfect obedience. This righteousness is counted, reckoned, or imputed to us by the forensic (that is, legal) declaration of God, as the sole ground of our justification. We deny that any works we perform at any stage of our existence add to the merit of Christ or earn for us any merit that contributes in any way to the ground of our justification" (Gal. 2:16; Eph. 2:8-9; Titus 3:5; GJC, 13).

8. Conclusion: Whether There Is a Consensual Protestant Teaching of Grace

A fair reading of these texts makes this conclusion clear: There is virtually no significant diversity in Protestant readings of the core teaching that we are saved by grace alone. Any attempt to show major disagreements is likely to be forced and tendentious. This does not imply that there are no differences of nuance or expression or historical context in these documents, but that within these various expressions there is an underlying ground of shared apostolic teaching. Even if some might argue there is hidden diversity in the particular language used in articulating the teaching of grace, that does not mean that there is no level of common consent embedded in them.

There are only two ways to challenge this consensus: Either (a) show that there are major unnoted inconsistencies between the core Protestant documents on justification by grace, or (b) show that there are other con-

45. DSWT 141.

sensual doctrinal standards that contradict or override this consensus. That would be a hard task for a challenger, and in my view would not be a successful challenge.

On this premise, what we still have ahead of us is demonstrating that this same teaching of salvation by grace alone was thoroughly understood by the most consensual of the ancient Christian writers before the Reformation. So we must, as the next chapter asserts, let the Fathers speak for themselves on *sola gratia*.

CHAPTER TWO

Let the Fathers Speak
for Themselves on Sola Gratia

"Grace alone" *(sola gratia)* is one of the central themes of the Reformers. They learned the radical priority of grace from the ancient Fathers, quoting them frequently as authorities on holy scripture. If this were widely known, the following section would be unneeded, but the sad truth is that it is seldom understood or referenced — either by modern liberals or evangelicals or Catholics or Orthodox — that the Fathers thoroughly understood justification by grace through faith. Hence this presentation of evidence.

The Fathers consensually understood that it is by grace alone that we are saved, not by works. This is proven repeatedly by their comments on Ephesians 2:4-10 and Romans 4, 5, and many others.

A. By Grace You Are Saved

In order further to develop and support these points, we now turn to the exegesis of key locus classicus passages on *sola gratia* that were thoroughly investigated by the Fathers.

1. The Fathers Teach That We Are Freely Justified as a Gift

Christians are not arrogant when they celebrate this salvation, since their faith, though a unique means of salvation, is not a work but is shaped by divine grace. "Do not rely on your own efforts," warned Ambrose, "but on the grace of Christ. 'You are,' says the apostle, 'saved *by grace*. Therefore it is not a matter of arrogance here but faith when we celebrate: we are accepted! This is not pride but devotion" (On the Sacraments 5.4.19).[1]

"What is 'the principle of faith'? This is salvation by grace. Here Paul shows God's power in that he has not only saved, he has also justified and led them to boast in a different way — not relying on works but glorying only in their faith" (Chrysostom, Homilies on Romans 7).[2]

"We have acquired the forgiveness of our former sins and have been justified freely by the mercy and grace of Christ" (Rom. 3:24; Cyril of Alexandria, Commentary on Romans).[3]

2. The Fathers Teach That Faith Alone Saves

The faithful are thus "justified by his grace as a gift, through the redemption which is in Christ Jesus" (Rom. 3:24). "They are justified freely," commented Ambrosiaster, "because they have not done anything nor given anything in return, but by faith alone they have been made holy by the gift of God" (Commentary on Paul's Epistles).[4]

"Paul is at great pains to show that faith is powerful to a degree which no one ever imagined the law could be," wrote Chrysostom. "For after saying that God justifies man by faith, he takes up the question of the law again. He does not say: 'Where are the good works of the Jews?' but: 'Where is their boasting?' Thus he takes every opportunity to demonstrate that it was all talk, and that they had no deeds to back them up. . . . In saying this, Paul is trying to get believing Jews to behave with moderation, and to reassure unbelieving Jews, so that they might be persuaded to accept his point of view. For if the one who has been saved is proud because he abides by the law, he will be told that he has stopped his own mouth, that he has accused himself, that he has renounced any claim to salvation and that he has excluded boasting. But the unbeliever may be humbled by these same means, and brought to accept the faith. See how great faith is, in that it has removed

1. CSEL 73:66; ACCS NT 9:133.
2. NPNF 1 11:378-79; ACCS NT 6:103.
3. PG 74 ad loc.; ACCS NT 6:104.
4. CSEL 81 ad loc.; ACCS NT 6:101.

us from the former things, and does not even allow us to boast of them!" (Homilies on Romans 7).[5]

The Fathers understood, along with Lutheran and Catholic peacemakers later, that "God justifies sinners in faith alone," and that "God himself effects faith as he brings forth such trust by his creative word" which "leads to a life in hope and love. . . . A distinction but not a separation is made between justification itself and the renewal of one's way of life that necessarily follows from justification and without which faith does not exist" (JD 4.3.26).

3. The Fathers Teach That Grace Is Unsearchable

God's gifts are unsearchable. What is known about them is precisely their unsearchability. "The divine Apostle says not only that Christ's nature is divine, but also that 'his riches are unsearchable.' 'And how does one preach if his riches are indeed unsearchable?' 'I preach this very thing,' he says, 'that they are unsearchable'" (Theodoret, Epistle to the Ephesians 3.8).[6]

It is precisely their mystery that has been made known in revelation. "'Unsearchable' and 'hidden' can be given two senses. The riches were previously unable to be searched out. They are now laid open after the Lord's passion. Another sense, perhaps even better: Those things which by nature were unsearchable to humanity are the ones that have been made known by God's revelation" (Jerome, Epistle to the Ephesians 2.3.8-9).[7]

The purpose of revelation is "to make all men see the plan of the mystery hidden for ages in God the Creator of all" (Eph. 3:9). The mystery of grace was largely, but not wholly, hidden in past ages. "The phrase *mystery hidden from the ages* could also be understood to mean that the very ages of time remained ignorant of his generosity when all spiritual and rational creatures who inhabited all previous ages remained unenlightened" (Jerome, Epistle to the Ephesians 2.3.8-9; cf. Gal. 1:4; Eph. 2:7).[8]

The mystery of grace is at work even when we do not recognize it, or recognize it only partially as within yet beyond our experience: "Our creator and dispenser so orders all things that love is increased when the di-

---

5. NPNF 1 11:378-79; ACCS NT 6:103.
6. CPE 2:19; ACCS NT 8:149.
7. PL 26:482C (593); ACCS NT 8:149.
8. PL 26:482D-483A (593-94); ACCS NT 8:150.

vine gifts which one does not see in himself are bestowed to be possessed by another. Thus the manifold grace of God is well dispensed when the gift received is believed to belong also to the one who does not have it and when it is believed to have been given for the sake of him with whom it is shared" (1 Pet. 4:10; Braulio of Saragossa, Letters 5).[9]

"In human terms, it was not possible for fishers to get the better of philosophers, but that is what happened by the power of God's grace" (Chrysostom, Homilies on the Epistles of Paul to the Corinthians 5.5).[10]

There is in natural religion a lack of adequate comprehension of the harmony that is between all the parts of the mystery of grace. This harmony is manifested in scripture. This harmony exists even if unseen. Its coherence is to be beheld in wonder. But it is grasped properly only by those who have been taught of God through the history of revelation. Reason when corrupted by sin can have little adequate understanding of grace.

This is why the mysteries of the gospel are considered folly from the perspective of reason unaided by grace. Reason, as corrupted by the history of sin, is suspicious of the mystery of grace. Religion itself easily becomes accommodated to corrupt reason.

4. The Fathers Teach That Grace Enables Freedom

"By the law comes the knowledge of sin; by faith comes the obtaining of grace against sin; by grace comes the healing of the soul from sin's sickness; by the healing of the soul comes freedom of choice; by freedom of choice comes the love of righteousness; by the love of righteousness comes the working of the law. Thus, as the law is not made void but established by faith, since faith obtains the grace whereby the law may be fulfilled, so freedom of choice is not made void but established by grace, since grace heals the will whereby righteousness may freely be loved" (Augustine, The Spirit and the Letter 52).[11]

Grace does not abolish free will. "By 'the grace of God,' Paul means the possession of every good thing. He is not excluding the role of free will by saying this, but teaching that every good work is made possible by the

9. FC 63:22; ACCS NT 11:117.
10. NPNF 1 12:25; ACCS NT 7:17.
11. LCC 8:236; ACCS NT 6:108.

help of God" (2 Cor. 8:1; Theodoret of Cyrrhus, Commentary on the Second Epistle to the Corinthians 327).[12]

B. The Fathers Teach That All Boasting Is Out of Place

1. *No Room for Boasting*

If salvation is by grace alone, its corollary is that there may be no boasting over works. To affirm that righteousness has been accounted us without merit is to rule out boasting over our own righteousness. Justification and boasting are opposite responses to grace. "Under the judgment of God the wisdom of the flesh can only blush at its miscalculations" (Ambrosiaster, Commentary on Paul's Epistles).[13]

God has not forbidden good works, but forbidden us to pretend to be justified by our good works. "God's mission," observed Chrysostom, "was not to save people in order that they may remain barren or inert. For Scripture says that faith has saved us. Put better: since God willed it, faith has saved us. Now in what case, tell me, does faith save without itself doing anything at all? Faith's workings themselves are a gift of God, lest anyone should boast. What then is Paul saying? Not that God has forbidden works, but forbidden us to be justified by works. No one, Paul says, is justified by works, precisely in order that the grace and benevolence of God may become apparent!" (Hom. on Ephesians 4.2.9).[14]

The Fathers commented extensively on Paul's exclusion of works-righteousness: "Then what becomes of our boasting? It is excluded. On what principle? On the principle of works? No, but on the principle of faith" (Rom. 3:27). "For who will glory, or for what, when everyone has become worthless and gone out of the right way, and nobody does good works any more? Therefore he says that all glorying is excluded," according to Cyril of Alexandria (Commentary on Romans).[15]

---

12. PG 82:422; ACCS NT 7:270.
13. CSEL 81:19-20; ACCS NT 7:18.
14. IOEP 2:140; ACCS NT 8:134.
15. PG 74 ad loc.; ACCS NT 6:104.

2. Glorifying God, Not Human Works

Good works may ironically become the occasion of harm for those tempted to boast in them. "Boasting, even if it is of good works, harms the soul of the boaster" (Theodore of Mopsuestia, Pauline Commentary from the Greek Church).[16]

There is a much great matter to celebrate than anything we can do for ourselves. For we can believe that God can do what we cannot do: "For the man who boasts in his works is boasting about himself, but the man who finds his honor in having faith in God has a much better reason for boasting, because he is boasting about God, not about himself. . . . To abstain from stealing or murder is a minor accomplishment, compared to believing that God can do the impossible" (Chrysostom, Homilies on Romans).[17]

The good news of Christ offers a challenge to all human pride. "Paul's intention is perfectly clear — to accost the pride of man, that no one should take glory in human works, and that no one should glory in himself" (Augustine, Predestination of the Saints 5.9).[18] "Paul shows clearly that righteousness depends not on the merit of man, but on the grace of God, who accepts the faith of those who believe, without the works of the Law" (Jerome, Against the Pelagians 2.7).[19]

What is being excluded is not perfect works only, but all works insofar as they are considered grounds for claiming justification before God. Excluded are not merely works that are accompanied by a conceit of merit, and not merely works done before believing, in the strength of our own wills, but all works insofar as they might pretend to contribute to our justification. This means not only the works of the ceremonial law are excluded, but also of the moral law when considered as a means of righteousness.

The Spirit works in the faithful to elicit good works. The Lutheran Formula of Concord would later echo the Fathers: "It is God's will and express command that believers should do good works which the Holy Spirit works in them, and God is willing to be pleased with them for Christ's sake and he promises to reward them gloriously in this and in the future life."[20]

---

16. NTA 15:174; ACCS NT 7:18.
17. NPNF 1 11:385-86; ACCS NT 6:110.
18. FC 86:228; ACCS NT 7:18.
19. FC 53:306; ACCS NT 6:106.
20. JD Annex, p. 46.

3. The Strength of Grace Works Precisely through Human Weakness

There is no room for boasting. "God chose what is foolish in the world to shame the wise, God chose what is weak in the world to shame the strong, God chose what is low and despised in the world, even things that are not, to bring to nothing things that are so that no human being might boast in the presence of God" (1 Cor. 1:27-29). "God did not just choose the unlearned, but also the needy, the contemptible and the obscure, in order to humble those in high places" (Chrysostom, Homilies on the Epistles of Paul to the Corinthians 5.3).[21]

God's grace is shown through utterly weak things, like the Nativity and the Cross. Writes Ambrosiaster: "The two most 'foolish things of the world' are in particular the virgin birth of Christ and his resurrection from the dead. The wise are confounded because they see that what a few of them deny, the many profess to be true. There is no doubt that the opinions of the many faithful take precedence over those of a small number. Likewise, those who are mighty in this world can easily see the so-called weak things of Christ overturning demons and performing miracles. To the world the injuries and sufferings of the Savior are weak things, because the world does not understand that they have become the source of power through Christ who submitted to suffering in order to overcome death" (Ambrosiaster, Commentary on Paul's Epistles).[22]

4. The Grace of Resurrection

"Since he rose," noted Theodoret, "we hope that we too shall rise. He himself [by his rising] has paid our debt. Then Paul explains more plainly how great the gift is: 'You are saved by grace.' For it is not because of the excellence of our lives that we have been called, but because of the love of our Savior" (Epistle to the Ephesians, 2.4.5).[23] "Therefore, as it is written, 'Let him who boasts, boast of the Lord'" (1 Cor. 1:31; cf. Jer. 9:24).

We are "created in Christ Jesus for good works" (Eph. 2:10b) in a new

---

21. NPNF 1 12:24; ACCS NT 7:18.
22. CSEL 81:18-19; ACCS NT 7:17.
23. CPE 2:12; ACCS NT 8:132.

creation, participating in the resurrection. Theodore of Mopsuestia commented: "[Paul] is speaking not of the first but of the second creation," the new creation in Christ, "wherein we are re-created by the resurrection. Completely unable as we are to mend our ways by our own decision on account of the natural weakness that opposes us, we are made able to come newly alive without pain and with great ease by the grace of the One who re-creates us for this purpose" (Epistle to the Ephesians 2.10).[24]

We are mercifully saved despite our unworthiness, through the resurrection of Christ. Without exception, all who are saved are saved by grace. The faithful are already in a sense raised to heaven through the resurrection of Christ. We can claim no credit for our conversion, or our subsequent good works. We can and must do works, but have no right to glory in them or in ourselves.

C. Grace in Action

1. How Grace Works

The entire plan of redemption is called a covenant of grace, which in time embraces, fulfills, and recasts the Mosaic covenant of works into a hymn of grace. Christ is the incarnate embodiment of grace to humanity, the Word become flesh, "full of grace and truth" (John 1:14). "For the law was given through Moses; grace and truth came through Jesus Christ" (John 1:17; cf. Eph. 2:7).

The law can point out ills, but not heal them. This happens only by grace: "Law without grace, then, can expose disease, but cannot heal. It can reveal the wounds but does not administer the remedy. But so that the law's precepts may be fulfilled, grace provides assistance within" (Gal. 3:22; Fulgentius, On the Truth of Predestination 1.41).[25]

We inherit the promises of God by grace (Rom. 4:16). Being heirs of grace (1 Pet. 3:7), the faithful are called to abound in gifts of grace (Acts 4:33; 2 Cor. 8:1). God's work is completed in the saints by grace (2 Thess. 1:11, 12). Grace is not given to be received in vain (2 Cor. 6:1). All of these texts received patristic comment consistent with Reformation teaching.

---

24. ACCS 8:135; *Catena Graecorum Patrum in Epistulas Pauli*, ed. J. Cramer (Oxford: Clarendon, 1854), 6:142.

25. CCL 91A:485 (980-83); ACCS NT 8:49.

"What then? Are we to sin because we are not under law but under grace? By no means!" (Rom. 6:15). Ambrosiaster begins his complex explanation by stating that "the Law is from God, so as to avoid possible opposition from someone who would make this objection. But if this is the case, why do we not have to be under it? Paul deals with this problem and teaches that by the will of God, who is the author of the Law, we have been set free from it by Christ. Although it was right for the Law to be given — for it was given in order to show that those who sinned against it were guilty before God and in order to dissuade people from continuing to sin — yet because of the weakness of its infirmity the human race was unable to restrain itself from sin and had become subject to the death of hell. God was moved by the righteousness of his mercy, by which he always comes to the aid of the human race, and through Christ he provided a way by which he could reward those who were without hope. By forgiving their sins he released them from the Law which had held them subject. Restored and made whole again by the help of God, they could reject the sins by which they had previously been held down. Therefore we did not sin in rejecting the Law but rather we followed the providence of God himself through Christ" (Ambrosiaster, Commentary on Paul's Epistles).[26]

2. Grace Can Only Be Received

No one has ever been born by asking parents for the opportunity to breathe. No one is there to do the asking. Precisely nothing exists before the zygote receives nascent life in conception. Before conception, there is not even a hint or glimpse or preliminary fantasy of the gift of life by which one might have imagined some hope or desire for life (John 3:3-8; Chrysostom, Hom. on John, 24, 25).[27] So with grace.

Although the Joint Declaration of Lutherans and Catholics does not attempt to ground itself primarily in patristic sources, it does conclude: "Together we confess: By grace alone, in faith in Christ's saving work and not because of any merit on our part, we are accepted by God and receive the Holy Spirit, who renews our hearts while equipping and calling us to good works" (JD 15). "Justification takes place solely by God's grace" (JD 17).

26. CSEL 81:203; ACCS NT 6:167-68.
27. FC 33:232-50.

The Joint Declaration redefines terms that have been divisive: "When Catholics say that persons 'cooperate' in preparing for and accepting justification by consenting to God's justifying action, they see such personal consent as itself an effect of grace, not as an action arising from innate human abilities. According to Lutheran teaching, human beings are incapable of cooperating in their salvation because as sinners they actively oppose God and his saving action. Lutherans do not deny that a person can reject the working of grace. When they emphasize that a person can only receive (mere passive) justification, they mean thereby to exclude any possibility of contributing to one's own justification, but do not deny that believers are fully involved personally in their faith, which is effected by God's Word" (JD 17). "The strict emphasis on the passivity of human beings concerning their justification never meant, on the Lutheran side, to contest the full personal participation in believing; rather it meant to exclude any cooperation in the event of justification itself. Justification is the work of Christ alone, the work of grace alone."[28]

What is said of the joint intention of Catholic and Protestant teaching of justification can also be said of the Fathers: "When Catholics emphasize the renewal of the interior person through the reception of grace imparted as a gift to the believer, they wish to insist that God's forgiving grace always brings with it a gift of new life, which in the Holy Spirit becomes effective in active love. They do not thereby deny that God's gift of grace in justification remains independent of human cooperation" (JD 4.2.24).

D. The Gift of Faith and Human Agency

In God's eyes we are self-determining persons. We are not mud balls to be thrown. Grace appeals to our freedom, seeking to engender free responsiveness.

The Spirit works to awaken the cooperation of human willing with God's own good will. "Through Jesus Christ the law of the Spirit of life set me free from the law of sin and death" (Rom. 8:2).

Grace enables the will voluntarily to believe. "The power to believe is the gift of God, but believing is an act of the creature, which is required as

28. VELKD 84, 3-8; JD 31.

a condition of pardon, and without which the sinner cannot obtain salvation" (Confession of the Free-will Baptists 1834).[29]

1. Faith Is a Gift Requiring a Response

Grace is ours to receive. "Just as a writing-pen or a dart has need of one to employ it, so also does grace have need of believing hearts. . . . It is God's part to confer grace, but yours to accept and guard it" (Cyril of Jerusalem, Catechetical Lectures, 1.3–1.4).[30]

In response to all that God has done, the hearer is invited to act so as to rely upon God's act. It is not asserted that faith can act by itself, but that it does, must, and will act responsively.

Faith's sufficiency is from God, yet so as to enable freedom, action, and trust. "This righteousness from God comes through faith in Jesus Christ to all who believe." All who have sinned "are justified freely by his grace through the redemption that came by Christ Jesus" (Rom. 3:22-24).

While justification is imputed, wholly as a gift, another step is required: for *what is imputed seeks to be imparted,* given in such a way that spiritual gifts can be appropriated as acts of freedom.

2. Grace and Active Willing

Faith is enabled as a gift of God without ceasing to be a free human act. God works in us that we may have a good will, and with us when we do have a good will (Augustine, On Nature and Grace).[31] Since "it is God who works in you," you are asked to "continue to work out your salvation" (Phil. 2:12, 13).

If faith is an act of trust, it requires a willing human agent — one made capable of trust. Faith trusts in the "author [ἀρχηγὸν] and perfecter [τελειωτὴν]" upon whom our eyes are fixed, "who for the joy set before him endured the cross" (Heb. 12:2).

God does not believe for us, but enables our believing. It is a highly

29. Ch. 10, 1868, COC 3:753.
30. FEF 1:348, sec. 808.
31. NPNF 1 4:121.

personal act of freedom to trust God. Faith is truly our own action, yet always enabled by grace, exercising the gracious ability God has given us to have full confidence in the eventful Word spoken in Jesus Christ.

As we receive food by eating, we receive Christ by believing (Helvetic Confession, XV).[32]

Augustine commented extensively on the relation of grace and will, and in particular on Philippians 2:12, 13: "It is not that the will or the deed is not ours, but without his aid we neither will nor do anything good" (On the Grace of Christ 26).[33] "It is certain that when we do a deed, the deed is ours; but he is the one who makes us do the deed by giving us strength fully sufficient to carry out our will" (On Grace and Free Will 32).[34] It is not within God's will that "anyone should be forced against his will to do evil or good but that he should go to the bad, according to his own deserts, when God abandons him. For a person is not good if he does not will it, but the grace of God assists him even in willing. It is not without cause that it is written, 'God is the one who works in you to will and to do, of his own good will'" (On Two Letters of Pelagius 1.36).[35] "We should not suppose, because he said, 'For it is God that works in you both the willing and the doing,' that he has taken away free will. For if that were so he would not have said above, 'Work out your own salvation with fear and trembling.' For when he bids them work, it is agreed that they have free will. But they are to work with fear and trembling so that they will not, by attributing the good working to themselves, be elated by the good works as though they were their own" (On Grace and Free Will 21).[36]

3. Receptive Faith and Its Activity;
Active Faith and Its Receptivity

Faith is neither passive waiting so as to lack activity nor compulsively acting so as to lack receptivity. Rather, it is a receptivity that acts responsively, and an activity that is fully accountable.

As *activity* in response to grace, faith acts through its receptivity. It

32. BOC 5.110.
33. PL 44:373; ACCS NT 8:258.
34. PL 44:900-901; ACCS NT 8:258.
35. PL 44:567; ACCS NT 8:258.
36. PL 44:894; ACCS NT 8:258.

gives through receiving. It walks through being held up. It speaks through being spoken to.

With faith as *receptivity*, the whole person stands in full readiness as if emptied of arbitrary self-will to receive and follow the Way of life.

Only one who is emptied of arbitrary self-will is ready to become filled with God's love and power. Only one fully receptive to God's Spirit becomes fully active in relation to neighbor. Faith is an activity that lives out of Christ, that knows and wills in Christ, a life of union with Christ.

The mystery of receptivity and activity repeatedly appears in the Pauline epistles: "So then, just as you received Christ Jesus as Lord, continue to live in him, rooted and built up in him, strengthened in the faith as you were taught" (Col. 2:6). "But whatever was to my profit I now consider loss, . . . that I may gain Christ and be found in him, not having a righteousness of my own that comes from the law, but that which is through faith in Christ — the righteousness that comes from God and is by faith" (Phil. 3:7-9).

The same receiving/acting or gift/task dynamic was rightly grasped by Luther: "Christ as a Gift nourishes your faith and makes you a Christian; but Christ as an Example exercises your works. These do not make you a Christian but are performed by you, who have previously been made a Christian" (Luther, Church Postil, 1522).[37] "Christ is set before us and given to us as an example and pattern which we are to follow. For when we possess Christ through faith as a free gift, we should go on and do as He has done for us and imitate Him in our entire life and sufferings" (Luther, Sermon on 1 Peter 4, 1523).[38]

While justification is imputed wholly as a gift, the gift itself seeks an active response: The justifying grace that is credited as a paid-up debt seeks to be appropriated in behavior through freedom.

"What does it mean to receive the grace of God in vain except to be unwilling to perform good works with the help of his grace?" (Caesarius of Arles, Sermon 126.5).[39]

The readiness dynamic is implied in the account of Peter's confession, "You are the Christ, the Son of the living God." For Jesus replied: "Flesh and blood has not revealed it unto you, but my Father who is in heaven" (Matt. 16:17).

---

37. WLS 1:199; WA 10 I, 1, 11f.
38. WLS 1:199; WA 12, 372.
39. FC 47:219; ACCS NT 7:254; cf. 2 Cor. 6:1.

E. The Grace of Effectual Calling

1. Preparing Grace Leads to Calling

God prepares the heart for the coming recognition of grace. The grace of calling *(gratia vocans),* or summoning grace, is a function of God's gracious preparing activity. The grace of calling and hearing is always a preparing grace that invites those buried in sin to awaken and rise to new life: "Wake up, O sleeper, rise from the dead, and Christ will shine on you" (Eph. 5:14).

Justification presupposes a preparing work of God's grace, which much of the Protestant tradition has termed "effectual calling." "Effectual calling is the work of God's Spirit (2 Tim. 1:9) whereby, convincing us of our sin and misery (Acts 2:37), enlightening our minds in the knowledge of Christ (Acts 26:18), and renewing our wills (Ezek. 36:26), he does persuade and enable us to embrace Jesus Christ freely offered to us in the gospel (John 6:44, 45)."[40]

"The Spirit applies to us the redemption purchased by Christ, by working faith in us (Eph. 2:8), and by it uniting us to Christ in our effectual calling (Eph. 3:17)."[41] Insofar as we respond to our calling in Christ, we "do in this life partake of justification (Rom. 8:30), adoption (Eph. 1:5), sanctification, and the various benefits which in this life do either accompany, or flow from them (1 Cor. 1:30)."[42]

2. Sufficient Grace

To the extent that we fall from grace, it is our own deficiency in receiving the sufficient grace given. To the extent that we return to receive grace, it is God's own act enabling our act.

We cannot turn to God except as God arouses and helps us to a good will. Yet when we turn away from God, we do so without the help of God, by our own absurd willfulness. For what have we that we have not received from God except evil?

---

40. Question 30, C. H. Spurgeon, *The Puritan Catechism.*
41. Question 29, C. H. Spurgeon, *The Puritan Catechism.*
42. Question 31, C. H. Spurgeon, *The Puritan Catechism.*

However viable the seed, it cannot sprout without sun and moisture. However active or assertive is human freedom, it cannot bear salutary fruit without being stimulated by the heat and moisture of God's own preparing grace (John 15:4).

F. New Life under Grace

1. *Dying to Sin, Living to God*

Can one who died to sin still live in it? "In order for this point to be clearer, let us inquire as to what it means to live to sin and what it means to die to sin. Just as living for God means living according to God's will, so living to sin means living according to sin's will, as the apostle says [in Rom. 6:12]. To live to sin therefore, means to obey the desires of sin. . . . Note how carefully Paul has weighed his words when he says: 'Can we still live in sin?' To go on in this way means to continue something without interruption. If someone does this it is clear that he has never been converted to Christ. But it sometimes happens not that someone continues in sin but that after having broken with it he goes back to his vomit and becomes most unfortunate, since after having rejected the rule of sin and death and accepted the rule of life and righteousness he returns to the control of sin and death. This is what the apostle calls the shipwreck of faith (1 Tim. 1:19)" (Origen, Commentary on the Epistle to the Romans 3:128, 132, 134).[43]

What does dying to sin and living to God mean? "To sin is to live to sin, and not to sin is to live to God. Therefore, when the grace of God through Christ and through faith came upon us, we began by the spiritual rebirth of baptism to live to God, and we died to sin, which is of the devil. This is what dying to sin means: to be set free from sin and to become a servant of God. Therefore, having died to sin, let us not go back to our earlier evils, lest by living once again to sin and dying to God we should incur the penalty from which we have escaped" (Ambrosiaster, Commentary on Paul's Epistles).[44]

What does it mean to be dead to sin in baptism? "Being dead to sin means not obeying it any more. Baptism has made us dead to sin once and

---

43. ACCS NT 6:153.
44. CSEL 81:191; ACCS NT 6:153.

for all, but we must strive to maintain this state of affairs, so that however many commands sin may give us, we no longer obey it, but remain unmoved by it, as a corpse does" (Chrysostom, Homilies on Romans 10).[45]

2. Dead in Trespasses, Raised Up with Christ

"Even when we were dead through our trespasses, [God] made us alive together with Christ (by grace you are saved), and raised us up with him, and made us sit with him in the heavenly places with Christ Jesus" (Eph. 2:5, 6).

God has already "raised us up with him" (Eph 2:6). "In the light of God's foreknowledge, Paul is speaking of what is to come as though it had already been done. . . . One who understands the resurrection and the kingdom of Christ spiritually does not scruple to say that the saints already sit and reign with Christ! Just as a person may become truly holy even in the flesh, when he lives in the flesh and has his conversation in heaven, when he walks on earth and, ceasing to be flesh, is wholly converted into spirit, so he is also seated in heaven with Christ. For indeed 'the kingdom of God is within us' (Luke 17:21)" (Jerome, Epistle to the Ephesians 1.2.1 seq.).[46]

Jesus was "put to death for our trespasses and raised for our justification" (Rom. 4:25; JD 13). Since we are already raised, we need not act as if dead. "What now seems nonsense to unbelievers then will appear as fully sensible to everyone. We will sit with him. Nothing is more trustworthy and worthy of praise than this revelation" (Chrysostom, Hom. on Ephesians 2.7).[47]

3. A Special Grace Is Given to the Humble

Grace is specially given to the humble (Prov. 3:34). "God gives grace to the humble" (James 4:6). We do well to draw near to those who are humble and learn from them. "Scripture says that God resists the arrogant but

---

45. NPNF 1 11:405; ACCS NT 6:153.

46. PL 26:468B-69A (574-75) following Origen, Epistle to the Ephesians, JThS 3:405; ACCS NT 8:132.

47. IOEP 4:139; ACCS NT 8:133.

gives grace to the humble. We should associate with those to whom God's grace has been given" (Clement, Letter to the Corinthians, 1.30.2-3).[48]

God resists the proud. "God punishes robbers, perjurers, gluttons and other sinners because they are in contempt of his commandments, but it is said that he resists the proud in a special way. This is because those who trust in their own strength, who neglect to submit themselves to God's power, who really think that they can almost save themselves and therefore have no time to seek help from above — these are all deserving of greater punishment. On the other hand, God gives grace to the humble because they recognize their need and ask him for help to overcome the plague of their sins, and for this reason they deserve to be healed. It ought to be noted that James quotes this verse from Proverbs according to the Septuagint, as does Peter in his letter. The Latin text, which is based on the Hebrew original, reads: 'Toward the scorners he is scornful, but to the humble he shows favor' (Prov. 3:34)" (Bede, Concerning the Epistle of St. James).[49]

Augustine was attentive to the special dangers in the path of one who appears to be "free from all vices and blemishes of conduct. For her I fear pride — I dread the swelling of self-conceit from so great a blessing. The more there is in her which she is satisfied with, the more I fear that in pleasing herself she will displease the one who resists the proud, but gives grace to the humble" (Augustine, *De sancta virginitate* 34).[50]

4. Freedom Undiminished by Grace

Faith does not diminish human freedom, but actualizes it. When Paul writes "by grace you have been saved through faith," explained Jerome, he "says this in case the secret thought should steal upon us that 'if we are not saved by our own works, at least we are saved by our own faith, and so in another way our salvation is of ourselves.' Thus he added the statement that faith too is not in our own will but in God's gift. Not that he means to take away free choice from humanity . . . but that even this very freedom of choice has God as its author, and all things are to be referred to his gener-

48. LCC 1:57; ACCS NT 11:47-48.
49. PL 93:33; ACCS NT 11:48.
50. FC 27:184-85; ACCS NT 11:48.

osity, in that he has even allowed us to will the good" (Epistle to the Ephesians 1.2.8-9).[51]

"Do we then make void freedom of choice through grace? God forbid! Rather, we establish freedom of choice. As the law is not made void by faith, so freedom of choice is not made void but established by grace. Freedom of choice is necessary to the fulfillment of the law" (Augustine, The Spirit and the Letter, 52).[52]

In this way, "The law is confirmed by faith. Apart from faith the law merely commands, and it holds guilty those who do not fulfill its commands, so that it might thereafter turn to the grace of the Deliverer those groaning in their inability to do what is commanded" (Augustine, Questions 66.1).[53]

The New Hampshire Baptist Confession of 1833, article 6, places responsibility upon the hearer for responding to the gospel: "Nothing prevents the salvation of the greatest sinner on earth but his own inherent depravity and voluntary rejection of the gospel; which rejection involves him in an aggravated condemnation."[54]

It remains our responsibility not to reject the gift of God. "The call of the gospel is co-extensive with the atonement to all men, both by the word and the striving of the Spirit; so that salvation is rendered equally possible to all. If any fail of eternal life, the fault is wholly their own" (Confession of the Free-will Baptists 1834, 1868, Ch. 7).[55]

The freedom to hear implies also the freedom not to hear, to decline the invitation. Some who are called "did not listen or pay attention; they were stiff-necked and would not listen or respond to discipline" (Jer. 17:23). Hence the imperative: "Today, if you hear his voice, do not harden your hearts" (Ps. 95:8).

5. Using without Abusing Grace

"What shall we say then? Are we to continue in sin that grace may abound? By no means! How can we who died to sin still live in it?" (Rom. 6:1-2). The thought of sinning that grace may abound is contradictory. "Whoever tries

51. PL 26:470 A-B; ACCS NT 8:133.
52. LCC 8:236; ACCS NT 6:107-8.
53. FC 70:140; ACCS NT 6:108.
54. COC 3:744.
55. COC 3:753.

to increase sin in order to feel an increase of grace does not understand that he is behaving in such a way that grace can do nothing in him. For the work of grace is that we should die to sin" (Augustine, On Romans 31.11, 13).[56]

Grace does not give us license to sin. "[Paul] is saying [in Rom. 6:15] that since we are free of sin we are no longer under the law. He does not mean that the outpouring of grace has given us license to sin" (Theodore of Mopsuestia, Pauline Commentary from the Greek Church).[57]

"Use your gifts" (1 Pet. 4:10). "It is not merely that the rich man is obliged to meet the needs of those who are less well off than he is but also that each one of us must use the gifts which we have received either by nature or by the Holy Spirit, so that no one may say that we are keeping these things to ourselves and refusing to share them with our neighbors" (Andreas, *Catena*).[58]

Pray that grace will be received and put to use without being abused (Rom. 3:8; 6:1, 15). To return to sin having received grace is to reject the kingdom. "The believer who returns to his former way of life rejects the kingdom of God's grace and returns to sin, i.e., to the pattern of his previous life. For we have received mercy for two reasons: first, that the kingdom of the devil might be removed, and second, that the rule of God might be proclaimed to the ignorant, for it was by this means that we came to desire this dignity" (Ambrosiaster, Commentary on Paul's Epistles).[59]

6. The Grace That Is Coming

The coming of grace in glory was foretold by the prophets. The gospel is an announcement of the coming of grace (Acts 20:24, 32). There is promised a special manifestation of grace at the end-time coming of Christ. You are called to "set your hope fully upon the grace that is coming" (1 Pet. 1:13).

The grace received by the prophets was the same in intention as that received by all believers. "The prophets inquired of the grace that was to be yours" (1 Pet. 1:10). The prophets "preached these things, knowing that they were not going to be revealed directly to them but would appear at

---

56. ACCS NT 6:153-54.
57. NTA 15:122-23; ACCS NT 6:168.
58. CEC 77; ACCS NT 11:117.
59. CSEL 81:189-91; ACCS NT 6:152.

some future time. Therefore it is wrong to say that their sanctification was somehow inferior to ours" (Didymus the Blind, Commentary on 1 Peter).[60] "The prophets inquired and sought out whatever information they could obtain from the Lord or from angels, in the secret recesses of their hearts, about the future grace of the gospel and about how and when eternal salvation would come into the world" (Bede, On 1 Peter).[61]

God "made us alive together with Christ . . . that in the coming ages he might show the immeasurable riches of his grace in kindness toward us in Christ Jesus" (Eph. 2:5, 7). "This grace was given, to preach to the Gentiles the unsearchable riches of Christ, and to make all men see the plan of the mystery hidden for ages in God who created all things" (Eph. 3:8b, 9).

Be ready at all times to receive this coming grace. "You must do this, Peter says, because you have been promised that you will see the revelation of Jesus Christ, which the angels now look upon, after your death. The greater the grace that has been promised to you, the more you ought to make sure that you are ready to receive it. You must be pure and chaste in your minds, waiting for the Lord to come, for if someone is unable to please God now, it is certain that he will not receive the reward promised to the righteous when Christ comes again" (Bede, On 1 Peter).[62]

The evidence has shown that there is a stable, explicit, consensual tradition of exegesis of Paul's teaching of grace firmly established a thousand years before Luther. Now we turn to the definition of faith.

60. PG 39:1757; ACCS NT 11:74.
61. PL 93:44; ACCS NT 11:74.
62. PL 93:45-46; ACCS NT 11:77.

PART THREE

BY FAITH ALONE

CHAPTER ONE

Justifying Faith

Only one step remains in this Reader, but it is a crucial completing step: we must discover for ourselves whether the Church Fathers understood *faith alone* in the same sense as did Luther and the Reformers.

Reprise: We have shown that the two complementary doctrines of justification and grace are classical consensual teaching for both patristic and Protestant sources. Our third and final step is to show how the classic teaching of faith is jointly shared by both old and new apostolic teachers. This completes the three parts of the Reader: 1. Justification 2. by grace 3. through faith.

Do the Protestant confessions generally agree on the nature of the faith that brings us into an upright and reconciled relation with God? Is there an underlying Protestant consensus on faith that is shared generally by virtually all Protestants, and is this grounded in the apostolic teaching of the ancient Christian writers? I will show the reasons for answering yes.

A. What Is Faith?

Faith (πίστις) is the means by which salvation is appropriated through personal trust in the Son as Savior.

The benefits of Christ's mediatorial work are applied by the Spirit and appropriated by the believer *through faith*. It is this faith that God declares as righteousness (Rom. 3:1–4:25; Augsburg Confession, Art. IV).

1. Faith Defined

Faith is the firm conviction (*persuasio,* Heb. 11:1) of the grace of God. Such faith is accompanied inwardly by the Spirit's assurance, and outwardly by works of love in relation to the neighbor. It is a firm "confidence *(fiducia)* of the heart, by which we *securely acquiesce* in the mercy of God promised to us through the gospel" (Calvin, CR XXXIII.333).[1] Faith elicits a sense of trusting repose in God who enables this conviction.

Faith is the primary condition set forth in scripture for receiving justification.[2] The jailer at Philippi was told by Paul: "Believe in the Lord Jesus, and you will be saved" (Acts 16:31). Faith is that act flowing out of true repentance which by grace trusts in Christ's righteousness.

2. Personal Trust

Saving faith is *personal trust* — trust in a person, Jesus Christ, the one mediator between God and humanity. The Greek terms that translate faith (πίστις, πιστεύω) imply reliance upon, trust in another who is experienced as trustworthy (root meaning: relying upon, binding, putting trust in).

Faith is less about Christ than in Christ. "Everyone who believes *in him* [εἰς αὐτόν] receives forgiveness" (Acts 10:43, italics added).

This personal trust is grounded in the conviction of the credibility of the apostolic testimony to him. "Anyone who believes in [πιστεύων εἰς] the Son of God has this testimony in his heart" (1 John 5:10). This testimony is the history of his coming, life, teaching, death, and resurrection. Faith in God assumes that God's disclosures about and of himself in the history of Jesus are true and sufficient for faith (Calvin, Inst., 2.6).

"Faith alone is the means and instrument whereby we lay hold on Christ the Savior, and so in Christ lay hold on that righteousness which is able to stand before the judgment of God. For that faith, for Christ's sake, is imputed to us for righteousness (Rom. 4:5)" (Lutheran Formula of Concord, Epitome of the Articles, 3.3).[3]

---

1. SHD II 402; cf. Inst. 3.1.1-7.
2. A. B. Bruce, KG, pp. 85-108; A. A. Hodge, OOT, pp. 465-81; A. H. Strong, ST, p. 465.
3. COC 3:116.

B. Faith Classically Defined in Hebrews 11:1

1. The Certainty of What We Do Not See

Both the Fathers and the Reformers commented extensively on the most straightforward definition of faith in the New Testament: "Now faith is being sure of what we hope for and certain of what we do not see" (Heb. 11:1).

By our living faith we demonstrate in life the reality of the things we cannot see. Our faith brings us to a kind of moral certitude in relation to what lies beyond physical sight. Faith requires laying hold of that which cannot be attained by sense perception or logic alone, but by trusting the person of Christ alone (Chrysostom, Homilies on Hebrews 22).[4]

Faith is our active, working confidence in and assurance of the truth of what we hope for. Faith itself elicits the evidence and conviction (ἔλεγχος) of that which cannot be seen (Luther, Lectures on Hebrews).[5] If revelation is the window to grace, faith is the eye that beholds it.

2. The Simplicity of Faith

In apostolic teaching, faith is utterly simple and direct. Christian teaching cannot do better than to convey that profound simplicity (Cyprian, Treatise XII).[6] Salvation comes through grace-enabled faith, not the absolute clarity of faith's attempts to define itself. "God was pleased through the foolishness of what was preached to save those who believe" (1 Cor. 1:21).

3. Risk-Taking Trust Is Required to Learn of Faith

In the classic Christian inquiry into faith one first prays for the grace to inquire rightly into faith (Augustine, Confessions, I.1).[7] Only if one is willing

---

4. NPNF 1 14:465.
5. LW 29:229ff.
6. ANF 5:547.
7. NPNF 1 1:45ff.

to risk following Christ by doing what he says will one then learn his doctrine (Chrysostom, Hom. on John, XLIX).[8]

Without choosing to follow in the Way, to hold to the Truth, and to live the Life, it is not likely that there will be sufficient readiness that saving grace will be rightly received and understood (Wesley, The Way to the Kingdom).[9] The meaning of faith is learned only through the obedience of faith.

The religious professionals were astonished that Jesus had such extraordinary learning "without having studied." Jesus made this extraordinary response: "If anyone *chooses* to do God's will, *he will find out* whether my teaching comes from God or whether I speak on my own" (John 7:17, italics added). The implication: Active, risk-taking trust is the required teaching arena in which one learns what faith in Christ is (Calvin, Inst. 1.14).

4. Faith's Evidences

Faith is distinguished from hypothesis, conjecture, supposition, fantasy, or imagination, because it is based upon the evidences of faith — revelation in history (John of Damascus, OF, III.9).[10] The task of faithful reasoning is to assess the quality of evidence.

To believe without evidence is gullibility. Faith is not gullible, since it does not require belief without evidence.

Faith looks for evidences in the actual fulfillment in history of God's promises. God teaches us by making promises and keeping his promises. This in part is an empirical search, but more profoundly a search for evidence in the flow of history. The evidence sought is more historical than laboratory or scientific in the narrow sense. Hebrews 11 provides a long list of such evidences in biblical prototypes of persons of faith.

To the extent that the evidence is historical it must be approached in the way that any historical evidence is rightly and appropriately established. The most profound historians are well aware of the limits of historical science if squeezed into a reductionist empiricist model.[11] The evi-

---

8. NPNF 1 14:177; Augustine, Comm. on John, Tractate XXIX.6, NPNF 1 7:184.
9. WJWB Sermon 7, 1:217-32.
10. NPNF 2 9:78.
11. See Wilhelm Dilthey, *Meaning in History,* and R. G. Collingwood, *The Idea of History.*

dences of faith are also moral, as Kant knew, hence they proceed by moral reasoning that constantly leaps the bounds of empirical evidence.[12]

5. Trusting beyond Sight without Doubt

God is not a visible object of sense. But by grace believers are made inwardly certain of what they cannot see or quantify empirically (John 1:18; Acts 17:29; Gregory Nazianzen, Orat.).[13]

Faith is distinguished from sight on the one hand, and doubt on the other. Believers walk by faith, which is distinguishable from both empirically certain sight and spiritually uncertain doubt. "We live by faith, not by sight" (2 Cor. 5:7). We walk by an inward seeing, even when outward seeing is constricted (John 6:40; Heb. 11:27). Faith "sees" (on the basis of previous fulfillments in the history of revelation) that which is mostly concealed from the sensory apparatus. It is "a trust in the unseen as though it were seen, in that which is hoped and waited for as if it were present" (Longer Catech., Eastern Orthodox Church, 6).[14]

Some outcomes of God's promise will always remain partially obscure until the end. Nonetheless, faith relies on the trustworthiness of God's providential love for the right ultimate unfolding of these outcomes.

The Letter to Hebrews celebrated the faith of Abel, Enoch, Noah, Abraham, and Moses: "All these people were still living by faith when they died. They did not receive the things promised; they only saw them and welcomed them from a distance" (Heb. 11:13). It is essential to living faith to trust what is unseen, or not completely seen, but revealed in such a way as to be understood as trustworthy even if not fully seen.[15]

6. The Condition for Receiving Justifying Grace

Faith is the only condition required for a reconciled relation to the Final Judge. Without faith no one can receive God's saving gifts.

---

12. *Critique of Pure Judgment, Prolegomena to the Metaphysics of Morals.*
13. NPNF 2 7:288-91.
14. COC 2:446.
15. Chemnitz, TNC, pp. 411-19, 450, 451.

Faith is the indispensable condition for receiving every subsequent stage of God's saving activity. It is the inward pivot of the Christian teaching of salvation (Luther, Freedom of a Christian).[16] At no point is it possible to say that having discussed faith, we can now turn to teach other subjects so as to leave faith behind (Calvin, Inst., 3.2).

The relation of righteous living and faith was grasped early in the Old Testament prophets. Habakkuk understood that "the righteous will live by his faith" (Hab. 2:4). Before him Jehoshaphat affirmed: "Have faith in the Lord your God and you will be upheld" (2 Chron. 20:20).

If it were intrinsically impossible for ordinary persons to believe in God, then faith could not be required as a duty, nor could unbelief be considered as sinful. Wherever a duty is seriously enjoined, the power to perform that duty must be reasonably implied.[17] That cannot be necessary which is impossible.

The power to believe is supplied by grace. It does not come by the fallen nature, or the alienated will acting autonomously. Were faith not enabled by preparing grace, then there could be no meaningful call to faith or guilt due to unbelief (Aphrahat, Demonstrations, On Faith).[18]

C. Justifying Grace Received Only by Faith

1. The Gift Requires a Response

Divine pardon is a gift that requires a response. It is a personal gift that must be received by a personal agent.

It is like a costly gift of love that hopes and calls for a response in order that it may be completely given and received (Wesley, The Way to the Kingdom).[19]

The benefits of justifying grace can be received only if they are received in trusting responsiveness. Faith's part is simply to acknowledge the rightness of God's act by receiving it trustingly, obediently (Ambrose, Of

---

16. MLS, pp. 56-61.
17. Kant, Prolegomena to the Metaphysics of Morals.
18. NPNF 2 13:350-52.
19. WJWB Sermon 7, 1:217-32.

Christian Faith, I.1ff.).[20] Faith praises the Justifier by taking seriously his costly, justifying action.

Taken by itself, repentance is not, strictly speaking, the pivotal condition of justification, but rather it is a necessary turning from wrongdoing that is presupposed in faith's reception of God's justifying action (Tertullian, On Repentance).[21]

2. Without Faith It Is Impossible to Please God

"Whoever does not believe stands condemned already" (John 3:18; Chrysostom, Hom. on John, XXVIII).[22] The world is being convicted of guilt "because men do not believe on me" (John 16:9; Augustine, Comm. on John, Tractate XCV).[23]

We place an insuperable obstacle in the way of our justification if we refuse to trust in God's mercy revealed on the cross. By voluntarily rejecting God's free gift, we leave ourselves at odds with God's way of winning us back. Without faith in Christ, there is no forgiveness of sins (Heb. 11:6; Acts 16:31; Mark 16:16). "Whoever rejects the Son will not see life" (John 3:36; Chrysostom, Hom. on John, 31).[24]

Every human action lacking trust in God, however well-intended, is fundamentally misguided. It is off the mark (hence ἁμαρτία, sin). What could be more offensive to God than to doubt the truth of God's costly suffering and death? Thus the absence of faith is viewed in the New Testament as a rejection of God's truth.

"Without faith it is impossible to please God, because anyone who comes to him must believe that he exists and that he rewards those who earnestly seek him" (Heb. 11:6). This very text then goes on to show that those who have not yet heard of Jesus Christ but believed in his promise can be justified by implicit, anticipatory faith in God's coming in Christ; their hearts are known only to God (Clement of Alexandria, Stromata, II.1-6).[25]

20. NPNF 2 10:201ff.
21. ANF 3:657ff.
22. NPNF 1 7:97.
23. NPNF 1 7:368-71.
24. NPNF 1 14:106.
25. ANF 2:347-54; cf. Calvin, Comm. XXII, pp. 270-82.

It is difficult to imagine how one could approach God without believing that God exists and that he rewards those who seek him. These two premises may be sincerely embraced by seekers even without hearing in detail of the history of Jesus. Without belief in the reality and justice of God, one can hardly approach further toward the mercy of God revealed.

Why doesn't God simply save everyone arbitrarily? "The reason that God does not save all is not that he wants the power to do it, but that in his wisdom he does not see fit to exert that power further than he actually does" (Auburn Declaration, 13).[26]

3. The Power of Faith

The gospel is "the power of God for the salvation of everyone who believes" (Rom. 1:16). In it "the righteousness of God is revealed through faith for faith" (Rom. 1:17; JD 12).

Even a little faith can have great power. Jesus attested the power of faith in dramatic terms: "If you have faith as small as a mustard seed, you can say to this mountain, 'Move from here to there,' and it will move. Nothing will be impossible for you" (Matt. 17:20).

What does seed have that makes it analogous to the kingdom of God? Readiness to receive the conditions of growth (Calvin, Comm. XVI, p. 326).

The greatness of God's power becomes clear when it brings life from death (1 John 4:7-21). Paul's preaching did not proceed "with wise and persuasive words, but with a demonstration of the Spirit's power, so that your faith might not rest on men's wisdom, but on God's power" (1 Cor. 2:5).

D. How Faith Is Congruent with Justification

1. Justifying Faith

What is justifying faith? The Westminster Larger Catechism states it clearly: "Justifying faith is a saving grace, wrought in the heart of a sinner, by the Spirit and word, in which he, being convinced of his sin and misery,

26. COC 3:779.

and of the disability in himself and all other creatures to recover him out of his lost condition, not only assents to the truth of the promise of the gospel, but receives and rests upon Christ and his righteousness therein held forth, for pardon of sin, and for the accepting and accounting of his person righteous in the sight of God for salvation" (Q. 72).

Key elements of justifying faith are summarized in the Baptist Confession of 1834: "Saving faith is an assent of the mind to the fundamental truths of revelation; an acceptance of the gospel, through the influence of the Holy Spirit; and a firm confidence and trust in Christ. The fruit of faith is obedience to the gospel" (Confession of the Free-will Baptists 1834, 1868, Ch. 10).[27]

2. Does Faith as Such Justify Apart from Grace?

Faith is the reception of grace. The simple unqualified phrase "justification by faith" is potentially distortable as the Reformers knew, insofar as it may be tempted to imply that our faith rather than God's grace saves (Calvin, Inst. 3.11-12). *The faithful are justified by grace, not by their own faith* (Melanchthon, Loci Communes).[28]

The Articles of Religion of 1615 of the Irish Episcopal (Anglican) Church clarify that "faith alone" does not imply faith without grace. "When we say that we are justified by faith only, we do not mean that the said justifying faith is alone in man without true repentance, hope, charity, and the fear of God (for such a faith is dead, and cannot justify). Neither do we mean that this, our act, to believe in Christ, or this, our faith in Christ, which is within us, of itself justifies us or deserves our justification unto us (for that would be to account ourselves to be justified by the virtue or dignity of something within ourselves)."[29]

3. Whether Faith Is a Condition of Salvation

Faith is called a "condition," not because it possesses any merit, but only because it is the single divinely chosen means, the only agency or instru-

---

27. COC 3:753.
28. LCC 19:89ff.
29. Article 36, COC 3:533.

ment by which the person appropriates Christ and his righteousness (Rom. 1:17; 3:25-26; 4:20-22; Phil. 3:8-11; Gal. 2:16).

Our participation is awakened through God's justifying initiative. "In order to stop anyone from asking: 'How can we be saved without contributing anything at all to our salvation?' Paul shows that in fact we do contribute a great deal toward it — we supply our faith!" (Chrysostom, Homilies on Romans 7).[30]

4. Faith Requires Renunciation, Freely Resolving to Live a Life of Righteousness

Faith requires a renunciation of all other pretended ways to God (Hos. 14:2, 3; Jer. 3:23; Ps. 71:16; Rom. 10:3), the consent of the will to this way (John 14:6), and the obedience of the heart to God (1 Pet. 1:21).

Faith freely resolves a life of righteousness grounded in the free gift of God's righteousness in Christ. This decision involves a renunciation of the devil and his powers, and all forms of idolatry.

But the will that must take this decisive step of renunciation is a will that has been trapped in idolatrous illusions. By its fallen nature this will is distrustful, self-assertive, and egocentric. This is why the broken will cannot begin to repent and have faith without grace enabling it (Augustine, On Forgiveness of Sins, and Baptism, II.5).[31] Conscience and reason, however distorted by sin, continue to try to attest that the person is constituted for communion with the eternal, invisible source and end of all things.

In chapter one we have defined faith and shown its congruence with God's justifying act on the cross. Now by following biblical prototypes of faith, we show how faith assents with the mind to the truth of the Word, consents with the whole will to surrender to the Word, and trusts with the heart in the living Word.

---

30. NPNF 1 11:377; ACCS NT 6:100.
31. NPNF 1 6:44-45.

CHAPTER TWO

Faith in God's Righteousness

A. Approaching God with Grounded Confidence

Faith frees the repentant sinner to approach God with confidence, by the
power of the Spirit. God the Spirit is providing sure and definite means of
grace to encourage the reconciled life: the pure preaching of the Word,
baptism, the Lord's Supper, daily scripture reading, worship, and pastoral
care.

1. Faith Is the Work of the Spirit

There is no saving faith without the work of the Holy Spirit: "Saving faith
is an intelligent and cordial assent to the testimony of God concerning his
Son, implying reliance on Christ alone for pardon and eternal life; and in
all cases it is an effect of the special operations of the Holy Spirit" (Auburn
Declaration, 11, 1837).[1]

"Where the Spirit of the Lord is, there is freedom" (2 Cor. 3:17b). The
Spirit yields freedom. "Because God is Spirit, he has given through Christ
the law of the Spirit, which persuades us to believe in invisible things
which our reasoning understands spiritually. This law gives liberty because

1. COC 3:779.

139

it demands only faith, and because it believes what it does not see, we are able to be rescued from our condition" (Ambrosiaster, Commentary on Paul's Epistles).[2]

2. Faith and the Means of Grace

The Spirit nurtures growing faith through the means of grace: "The grace of faith, whereby the elect are enabled to believe to the saving of their souls, is the work of the Spirit of Christ in their hearts, and is ordinarily wrought by the ministry of the Word, by which also, and by the administration of the sacraments, and prayer, it is increased and strengthened" (Westminster Confession, Ch. 14).[3]

God offers the outward means of grace and expects their diligent use: "He requires of us repentance towards God, and faith towards our Lord Jesus Christ, and the diligent use of the outward means whereby Christ communicates to us the benefits of his mediation" (Westminster Larger Catechism, Q. 153).

Baptism is the prototypical moment in which the confession of faith is made. This confession is repeatedly reaffirmed in the Christian life. "This condition is fulfilled at the time of baptism, when faith and profession of faith are all that is demanded for one to be baptized" (Augustine, The Christian Life).[4] What is professed at baptism? "This profession of faith is the Creed which you will be going over in your thoughts and repeating from memory" (Augustine, The Creed).[5]

Lutherans and Catholics jointly declared in 2000 that "The justified live by faith that comes from the Word of Christ (Rom. 10:17) and is active through love (Gal. 5:6), the fruit of the Spirit (Gal. 5:22f.). But since the justified are assailed from within and without by powers and desires (Rom. 8:35-39; Gal. 5:16-21) and fall into sin (1 John 8, 10), they must constantly hear God's promises anew, confess their sins (1 John 1:9), participate in Christ's body and blood, and be exhorted to live righteously in accord with the will of God" (JD 14). Lutherans and Catholics may now "confess to-

---

2. CSEL 81:219; ACCS NT 7:225.
3. Of Saving Faith, 4.1, CC, p. 209.
4. FC 16:36.
5. FC 27:289.

gether that in baptism the Holy Spirit unites one with Christ, justifies, and truly renews the person. But the justified must all through life constantly look to God's unconditional justifying grace" (JD 4.4.28).

3. Gaining Confidence in Approaching God

The Belgic Confession, 1561, stated the basis of our confidence in approaching the holy God: "We always hold fast this foundation, ascribing all the glory to God, humbling ourselves before him, and acknowledging ourselves to be such as we really are, without presuming to trust in any thing in ourselves, or in any merit of ours, relying and resting upon the obedience of Christ crucified alone, which becomes ours when we believe in him. This is sufficient to cover all our iniquities, and to give us confidence in approaching God; freeing the conscience of fear, terror, and dread, contrary to following the example of our first father, Adam, who trembling, attempted to cover himself with fig-leaves."[6]

As the act of faith secures our pardon, it looks also toward our sanctification. God's justifying verdict rightly received by faith does not lead to licentiousness (Rom. 6:2-7). Although our good works are not the ground of this Judge's pardon, they certainly are expected to follow from it (Rom. 6:14; 7:6).

Such faith brings abundant blessings (Ps. 32:1, 2; Rom. 4:6-8) because it frees from condemnation (Rom. 8:33, 34), and entitles the faithful to an inheritance (Titus 3:7).

4. Confess with the Lips What Is Believed in the Heart

"If you confess with your lips that Jesus is Lord and believe in your heart that God raised him from the dead, you will be saved. For man believes with his heart and so is justified, and he confesses with his lips and so is saved" (Rom. 10:9, 10).

"Take for instance that thief who was crucified next to Christ and who confessed Christ with his heart and his mouth (the two parts of him which were free; cf. Luke 23:42) and thus deserved to hear the reply: 'Today

6. Article 23, COC 3:408.

you will be with me in Paradise' (Luke 23:43)" (Anonymous, The Holy Letter of St. Paul to the Romans).[7]

How is belief with the heart related to confession with the lips? Can one believe anonymously, silently, without others knowing it? If called to a moment of required confession or denial of Christ under compulsion of civil authorities, can the believer keep silent? Augustine took a rigorous view of this: "Did not almost all those who disowned Christ in the presence of their persecutors keep in their hearts what they believed about him? Yet, for not making with their mouth profession of faith unto salvation they perished, except those who repented and lived again" (Augustine, Against Lying 6.13).[8]

The martyr, Ignatius of Antioch, emphatically lived out the truthful correspondence between heart and lips. "It is better for a man to be silent and be a Christian than to talk and not be one. . . . Men believe with the heart and confess with the mouth, the one unto righteousness, the other unto salvation. It is good to teach, if the teacher also does what he says" (Ignatius, Epistle to the Ephesians 15).[9]

The twin trumpets of heart and mouth must sound in harmony. "With these twin trumpets of heart and mouth we arrive at that holy land, viz., the grace of resurrection. So let them always sound together in harmony for us, that we may always hear the voice of God. Let the utterances of the angels and prophets arouse us and move us to hasten to higher things" (Ambrose, On the Death of His Brother Satyrus 2.112).[10]

"The understanding must be strongly fixed in pious faith and the tongue must herald forth by its confession the solid resolution of the mind" (Chrysostom, Baptismal Instructions 1.19).[11]

God knows the heart: "The Scripture says: 'No one who believes in him will be put to shame' (Isa. 28:16)" (Rom. 10:11).

The ambiguities of false teaching will not be made absolutely clear until the last day, when the final test of faith will occur: "On the day of judgment, when everything will be examined and all false opinions and teachings will be overthrown, then those who believe in Christ will rejoice, seeing it revealed to all that what they believed is true and what was

---

7 ENPK 2:73; ACCS NT 6:277.
8 FC 16:139; ACCS NT 6:276.
9. ANF 1:55; ACCS NT 6:275.
10. FC 22:249; ACCS NT 6:275-76.
11. ACW 31:30, ACCS NT 6:276.

foolish was wise. For they will look at others and see that they alone are glorified and wise, when they had been considered contemptible and crazy. This will be the real test, when rewards and condemnation are decreed (cf. Matt. 12:36-37)" (Ambrosiaster, Commentary on Paul's Epistles).[12]

5. Whether There Is a Patristic Consensus

I do not claim that the patristic justification teaching we see in the exegesis of Paul's letters was never abused or always rightly remembered or consistently appropriated. But the claim of some Protestants that it was never grasped or understood by any pre-Protestant teacher is evidently exaggerated.

I do not claim that the patristic teaching of justification by faith was always rightly integrated into preaching and pastoral care and moral instruction, but that is the case for Protestant teaching as well.

I do not claim that the patristic justification teaching was everywhere grasped in a full or perfect way, but I do claim that it was an ecumenical teaching, taught wherever Paul's letters were rightly taught and commented upon seriously.

The patristic teaching of justification was embodied and dramatized at the Lord's table. We learn it both from preaching and worship. This can be shown from the history of liturgy (in a way that goes beyond our present scope, but could be investigated in writers like Dom Gregory Dix, Louis Bouyer, Georges Florovsky, Alexander Schmemann, J. A. Jungmann, Jean Daniélou, and Geoffrey Wainwright). Arguably justification teaching is as explicit in the fifth century of the East and West than is present in some typical praise worship today. Most of the justification teaching metaphors were presented every Lord's Day to the early church through the continual reading of the scripture and through the liturgy of the body and blood of the Lord. More scripture was read in the ordinary church services and daily lectionaries of Gregory the Great's time than in many modern Protestant services. A case can be made that ancient Christian worship more consistently presented this doctrine in and through its liturgy than many Protestant churches do today, with all our bravado about how central is our justification teaching.

But did patristic teachers make an adequate evangelical and mis-

---

12. CSEL 81:349; ACCS NT 6:276-77.

sional appropriation of justification teaching? That awaited a much deeper exploration in the sixteenth century with Luther and Calvin, and eighteenth- and nineteenth-century evangelical revivalism. Despite knowing clearly the Pauline teaching of justification, the patristic teachers did not find adequate ways of presenting it and implementing it in their daily teaching and preaching. But they indeed did preach it, as shown in the preaching of Chrysostom, Ambrose, Augustine, Cyril of Alexandria, Theodoret, and Caesarius of Arles, and probably did that about as much as in modern Protestant preaching. The laity of that time, not having scriptural commentaries easily accessible, largely met the teaching of justification even more powerfully in their liturgical and iconographic experience, more as an act of beholding and experiencing than hearing and reading.

In what follows we will ask more explicitly: Can we establish textually that there is a pre-Protestant ancient Christian teaching of faith that corresponds with the consensual Protestant teaching? I will show that many patristic texts set forth the same essential understanding of faith that was received as the center of the Protestant tradition. It was thoroughly familiar to and accessible to the ancient Christian writers.

But there remains another level of complexity: Can this pre-Protestant teaching of faith that corresponds with consensual Protestant teaching be shown itself to be consensual? Despite occasional abuses and distractions, this ancient understanding of faith can, I think, be shown to be classic consensual teaching, as confirmed by councils and the major ecumenical doctors East and West. This validation can be established only by examining texts of scripture and tradition that exhibit it, which is our next task.

B. Biblical Examples of Faith

1. Faith as Exemplified by Abraham

"What then shall we say about Abraham, our forefather according to the flesh?" (Rom. 4:1).

Abraham is the model of faith in the history of salvation. This is seen in his forsaking the land of his birth upon the command of God (Gen. 12:1-4), in believing in the promise of many descendants (Gen. 12:7; 15:4-8), and in the readiness to offer up Isaac (Gen. 22:1-10; Rom. 4:18-21; Heb. 11:8-19). Among other biblical examples of faith are Noah, in building the ark (Gen.

6:14-22; Heb. 11:7), Joseph, in trusting God's providence while being sold into slavery (Gen. 50:20; Heb. 11:22), Moses, in the exodus (Heb. 11:24-28), Caleb, in advising to take the land of promise (Num. 13:30; 14:6-9), Rahab, in her hospitality to the spies (Josh. 2:9, 11; Heb. 11:31), and David, in believing God's promise that his kingdom would be a perpetual kingdom (Acts 2:30). Augustine, Cyril, Ambrose, Jerome, and others commented extensively on these faith texts.

Abraham trusted in God, not in his own doubts. "Since Abraham, without the law, obtained glory not by the works of the law (as if he could fulfil the law in his own strength); since the law had not yet been given, the glory belongs to God, not to him. For he was justified not by his own merit, as if by works, but by the grace of God through faith" (Augustine, On Romans 20, 7).[13]

Abraham's faith was implicitly a faith in the promise of God's future deliverance (Gregory of Nyssa).[14] Yahweh promised Abraham that all nations were to be blessed through his son, Isaac. Yet Yahweh commanded Abraham to go to Mount Moriah and offer up Isaac as a sacrifice! Abraham nonetheless trusted God, made his necessary preparations, and immediately set out on the journey. This exemplary readiness to trust in God's promise made him the prototype for all persons of faith in the Bible (Heb. 11:8-19).[15]

Before the call to sacrifice Isaac, Abraham already believed that all things are possible with God. "What can we say to those who insist that Abraham was justified by works because he was ready to sacrifice his son Isaac on the altar? Abraham was already an old man when God promised him that he would have a son and that his descendants would be as countless as the stars of the sky. Abraham piously believed that all things are possible with God and so exercised this faith. God reckoned him to be righteous on this account, and gave Abraham a reward worthy of such a godly mind, viz. the forgiveness of his previous sins. . . . So even if Abraham was also justified by his willingness to sacrifice Isaac, this must be regarded as an evident demonstration of a faith which was already very strong" (Cyril of Alexandria, Explanation of the Letter to the Romans).[16]

13. ACCS NT 6:110.

14. FGG 119-21.

15. Cf. Origen, Hom. on Gen. 8.5-6, FC 71:140-43; Ambrose, On Satyrus, 2.97, FC 22:240-44; Caesarius, Sermon 84.2-5, FC 47:16-19; Kierkegaard, F&T.

16. PG 74:780-81; ACCS NT 6:110.

2. Righteousness Was Accounted to
Abraham Due to His Faith Alone

"For what does the Scripture say? 'Abraham believed God, and it was reckoned to him as righteousness'" (Rom. 4:3; cf. Gen. 15:6). "Abraham believed God. Let us also believe, so that we who are the heirs of his race may likewise be heirs of his faith" (Ambrose, On the Death of His Brother Satyrus 2.89).[17]

"[Abraham] was already justified before he was circumcised" (Ambrosiaster, Commentary on Paul's Epistles).[18] "Paul revealed that Abraham had glory before God not because he was circumcised nor because he abstained from evil, but because he believed in God. For that reason he was justified, and he would receive the reward of praise in the future" (Ambrosiaster, Commentary on Paul's Epistles).[19]

"Was Abraham justified just because he had the faith to believe that he would be given a son? Or was it also because of all the other things which he had believed previously? . . . Before this point, Abraham had believed in part but not perfectly. Now, however, all the parts of his earlier faith are gathered together to make a perfect whole, by which he is justified" (Origen, Commentary on the Epistle to the Romans).[20]

The Marcionite challenge (extreme Paulinism) was an even greater problem for the early Fathers than was Judaizing (extreme legalism) on the other side. Irenaeus (A.D. 120-202) refuted Marcion for excluding Abraham from salvation in Christ: "Vain, too, are Marcion and his followers when they seek to exclude Abraham from the inheritance, to whom the Spirit through many men, and now by Paul, bears witness, that 'he believed God, and it was imputed unto him for righteousness'" (Irenaeus, Against Heresies 4.8.1).[21]

3. Distinguishing Implicit from Explicit Faith

Those who lived before Christ or who could not yet have explicitly heard the detailed history of the good news, may, by God's unsearchable mercy, share in an implicit faith in the promise of God's coming, even without

17 FC 22:236; ACCS NT 6:111.
18. CSEL 81:127; ACCS NT 6:109.
19. CSEL 81:129; ACCS NT 6:111.
20. CER 2:166, 168; ACCS NT 6:111.
21. ANF 1:470*.

grasping all the particulars of historical revelation. Such faith is efficacious, or "counted for righteousness," as in the case of Abraham (Rom. 4:5; Heb. 11:8-19). If Abraham came before Christ, yet believed in his future coming by faith, he may be said to hold an implicit faith.

This distinction was refined by the Reformers: Explicit faith (*fides explicita*) is an express belief in the truth of revelation in Jesus Christ, while *fides implicita* is a virtual belief, when one implicitly affirms by way of anticipation what the apostolic teaching would later teach, even if one may not fully understand it).[22] The lead text for this distinction is Hebrews 11.

The ancient patriarchs and prophets, who had implicit faith in Christ, were justified without explicit faith in the Trinity and Incarnation and without baptism. According to Hebrews 11, they believed in an anticipative sense through their eager longings and desires in a way that anticipated explicit faith even when it was not fully articulated or available to them.[23] To the extent a given person is capable of assent, implicit faith assents to at least two teachings presupposed in Hebrews 11:6: the existence and justice of God.

Long before Luther, Jerome had argued that the patriarchs, prophets, and saints before Christ were justified by the expectancy of their faith, anticipating the coming of Christ. "Some say that if Paul is right in asserting that no one is justified by the works of the law but from faith in Christ, the patriarchs and prophets and saints who lived before Christ were imperfect. We should tell such people that those who are said not to have obtained righteousness are those who believe that they can be justified by works alone. The saints who lived long ago, however, were justified from faith in Christ, seeing (John 8:56) that Abraham saw in advance Christ's day" (Jerome, Epistle to the Galatians 1.2.16).[24]

Faith acknowledges and celebrates the kindness of God. "The accomplishment of good works honors those who do them, but it does not reveal the kindness of God. Faith, on the other hand, reveals both the love for God of the one who believes, and God's kindness" (Theodoret of Cyrrhus, Interpretation of the Letter to the Romans, PG 82:88).[25]

---

22. Luther, On the Creed, Commandments and Lord's Prayer; Calvin, Inst. 3.2.3.
23. Calvin, SW, pp. 381-84; Inst. 3.2.10.
24. PL 26:343C-D (412); ACCS NT 8:30.
25. ACCS NT 6:110-11.

C. Classic Distinctions Regarding Faith

1. *Saving Faith Distinguished from General Human Faith*

Saving faith is full and unconditional reliance on Christ for salvation. It is an act of personal trust in the only true Mediator. Saving faith believes and personally trusts that Jesus is "the Christ, the Son of God" (John 11:27). Saving faith renounces all gods but the living God, disavowing all lords but the crucified-resurrected Lord, and is willing to take up one's cross and follow.

Some preliminary forms of inchoate faith indeed may appear in general human experience, according to scripture. The experience of trust is familiar to human experience of all cultures. It is not an exclusive possession of Christianity. Children trust parents. Students trust teachers to tell them the truth. Business transactions depend on trust in the currency. This common human experience is sometimes called *human faith* to distinguish it from that faith in Christ that is enabled by saving grace, which is termed *saving faith (fides salvifica),* or divine faith.

Conscience is a faculty of human consciousness that is formed in all human beings at some inchoate level, yet may become itself transformed by converting grace. A general human form of faith is seen in a capacity to believe in what is unseen. That is found universally in some form in the human condition, which may become enlivened by converting grace.

"Accordingly, the *capacity to have faith,* as the capacity to have love, belongs to men's nature; but *to have faith,* even as to have love, belongs to the grace of believers" (Augustine, On the Predestination of the Saints, 5:10).[26]

Saving faith in Christ must be distinguished from projection of human need or imagination. The Freudian teaching that some ideas of God are a projection of human needs (borrowed from Feuerbach) had been long before anticipated by Luther: "Faith is not man's opinion and dream, which some take to be faith. . . . When they hear the Gospel, they immediately devise from their own powers the imagination in their hearts to which they give expression in the words 'I believe.' This they regard the right faith. Nevertheless it is nothing but man's thought and imagina-

---

26. NPNF 1 5:503, italics added.

tion."[27] The dynamic of projection is not a modern idea but is frequently anticipated in classic exegesis. (See Lactantius, Divine Institutes, II.7.)[28]

2. General Faith and the History of Religions

Faith in God (in its intuitive, conceptual, discursive, human, and inchoate senses) belongs not just to the history of revelation but more generally to the history of religions. For God has not left himself without witness in the world (Acts 14:17).

An embryonic form of faith in God may be experienced in an anticipatory sense in the worship and sacrifice that godly and devout persons of all times have sought to offer to God, Abel being the prototype. God in time becomes known in creation and providence and general revelation, while the history of sin is being readied for God's personal self-disclosure in Jesus Christ.

"By faith we understand that the universe was formed at God's command, so that what is seen was not made out of what was visible" (Heb. 11:2). Such faith enters into a general human and rational understanding. It was "by faith" that "Abel offered God a better sacrifice," hence "by faith he still speaks, even though he is dead" (Heb. 11:4). "By faith Enoch was taken from this life" (v. 5).

Scripture is clearly signaling that those who lived prior to Christ and without historical knowledge of the yet-to-unfold history of salvation still could be saved by faith in the promise of that unfolding, insofar as God's mercy had been grasped by them in some anticipative way through reason, conscience, providence, social processes, and human religious traditions. It is for God, who knows the heart, to judge, and not for us, as to whether such faith may be efficacious for salvation.

The faith of non-Israelites was clearly of special concern to Jesus: "Other sheep I have, which are not of this fold" (John 10:16 KJV). Commenting upon the faith of the Roman centurion, Jesus said: "I tell you the truth, I have not found anyone in Israel with such great faith. I say to you that many will come from the east and the west, and will take their places

---

27. SCF, p. 188; cf. Luther, Large Catechism, I, BOC, p. 365.
28. ANF 7:50; cf. Athenagoras, A Plea in Defense of the Faith, 27, 28, LCC 1:330-31.

at the feast with Abraham, Isaac and Jacob in the kingdom of heaven" (Matt. 8:10, 11).[29]

3. The Possibility of Faith

Faith in the general religious sense is the faculty of accepting the unseen as true, and listening beyond the senses. Such a general faith knows what it knows without the empirical evidence ordinarily expected of knowledge of the material, physical world (Luther, Large Catechism, I).[30]

Saving faith does not require a new faculty of the self. Rather, the preparatory work of grace moves within human knowing, feeling, and willing to draw the person toward that saving faith which knows, feels, and wills in relation to God's own personal coming.

The preliminary capacity for personal trust is providentially encouraged by common grace. Every rationally matured human being has not only conscience, but also a latent sufficient capacity of intellect, sensibility, and will to be able to respond to grace when grace becomes known through the Word (Augustine, Confessions).[31]

"To whatever extent the truths of religion are known and embraced, faith in them is the healthy and legitimate exercise of the human mind, receiving the evidence, internal and external, which authenticates revelation" (Pope, Compendium of Christian Theology 2:377).

The faculty for faith, the possibility of trusting in God, is primitively present in every human spirit, everybody in-breathed to life by God. Despite the recalcitrance of sin, this faculty is gradually, through revelation, in God's own time, being awakened by God's own Spirit, always looking toward his decisive coming in Christ. Meanwhile, the capacity for faith may to some extent lie dormant.

Hilary of Poitiers brilliantly applied this analogy: "Just as a faculty of the human body will be idle when the causes that stir it into activity are not present, so with the soul. The eyes will not perform their functions except through the light or the brightness of day. The ears will not comprehend their task when no voice or sound is heard. The nostrils will not be

---

29. Irenaeus, Against Heresies, 4.58.10, AEG 2:311.
30. BOC, p. 365.
31. I.1, LCC 7:7.

aware of their office if no odor is detected. It is not that the faculty is lost because the cause is absent. Rather the employment of the faculty comes from the cause. It is the same with the soul of man. If the soul has not breathed in the gift of the Spirit through faith, even though it will continue to possess the faculty for understanding, it will not have the light of knowledge" (Hilary of Poitiers, Trinity 2:35).[32]

4. Faith as Believing and Believed

The faith that is believed is the apostolic testimony, the consensually received objective truth of the Christian faith *(fides quae creditur)*. This is the faith to which Jude referred when he urged his hearers to "contend for the faith that was once for all entrusted to the saints" (Jude 3).

That is different from the personal *act of believing* that truth personally and inwardly from the heart. That was called "faith actively believing" *(fides qua creditur,* faith as personally trusting in another).

So faith is both believed and actively believing. Faith can believe because it has heard of the faith that is believed (Irenaeus, Fragments, 34).[33]

The ancient Christian writers, just like the Reformers, found it useful and necessary to make precise distinctions in claims relating to justifying faith: They distinguished immature from mature faith active in love. They were clearly aware of the difference between human faith or general trusting in something (including historical faith and intellectual assent) and divine faith made possible by grace. They distinguished the apostolic faith that is believed from faith as believing. They understood that the study of faith (discursive faith) is distinguishable from the act of faith (or direct faith). They distinguished implicit from explicit faith. These indeed are distinctions made in Protestant orthodoxy, but they are also found in the exegetes of the early Christian centuries.

---

32. FC 25:63; ACCS NT 7:120.
33. ANF 1:574.

5. Contending for the Faith

Jude 3 calls us to contend for the faith once for all delivered to the saints. "The faith was first delivered to these people by the apostle Paul, who said: 'No other foundation can anyone lay, than the one which is already laid' (1 Cor. 3:11)" (Hilary of Arles, Introductory Commentary on Jude, PL *Supp.* 3:129).[34]

"Here Jude reveals what the purpose of his letter is. He is concerned for the salvation of those to whom he is writing and is afraid that in their naïveté they might be seduced by false teachers. In order to combat them, Jude will go on to expose their teachings. Peter had already done the same, but now Jude would give them a fuller exposition. Both Peter and Paul had predicted that such people would appear in the church, and even Christ himself had said: 'Many will come in my name and will lead many astray' (Mark 13:6)" (Theophylact, Commentary on Jude).[35]

Jude contends for the faith against ungodly persons who would pervert grace into license (Jude 4). "There are some godless men who twist Scripture wickedly and who have come into the church, pretending to preach the gospel. Their judgment was decreed long ago, and they have condemned themselves by their actions. As a result, they have been handed over to their impure lusts. By their great ungodliness they have turned the grace of our Lord Jesus Christ into wantonness, and by their wickedness even people who have been called by the gospel have denied the one Lord Jesus Christ. It is in order to win them back that Jude goes on to talk of what God did in the past to people who behaved in that way" (Didymus the Blind, Commentary on Jude).[36]

6. How Saving Faith May Be Studied

Saving faith may be temporarily taken out of its own realm of active trust in God in a community of worship, and subjected to rational analysis and reflection, as any other subject can be investigated. Saving faith can become the subject of academic definition or debate or public discourse.

34. ACCS NT 11:249.
35. PG 126:89; ACCS NT 11:249.
36. PG 39:1813; ACCS NT 11:249.

Faith in this sense is sometimes called *discursive faith,* or faith as a subject of intelligent discourse, as distinguished from a *direct faith* that actively trusts. It is direct faith that is being investigated, but in the process of investigation it temporarily becomes discursive faith.

Faith in the most general sense of its usage may rightly be viewed as a premise of all human knowing, all empirical inquiry, all deductive reasoning (Clement of Alexandria, Stromata, II.4, ANF 2:350). "For a farmer does not plow a furrow in the earth without faith, nor a merchant entrust his life to a bit of wood on the raging high seas. Neither are marriages contracted nor anything else in life done without faith" (John of Damascus, OF, Book IV.11).[37]

Moreover, one cannot make a scientific investigation without assuming the intelligibility of the natural order, an axiom that cannot be empirically proved. Hence when Anselm said: "I believe in order to know" (*credo ut intelligam*) he was expressing a scientific axiom that has with time become sadly less familiar to many modern scientists.

7. Historical Faith and Intellectual Assent

Saving faith in Christ is distinguishable from historical faith *(fides historica),* that faith which is convinced by historical evidence that an event occurred. One may believe on the basis of historical testimony that Christ in fact died on the cross, and yet not believe that his death was a ransom for one's own sin. Saving faith "is not merely a knowledge of historical events, but is a confidence in God" (Augsburg Confession, XX).[38]

Faith as personal trust is not sufficiently understood as merely a historical belief in the facts reported in scripture *(fides historica),* yet faith willingly hears the evidences of God's revelation in scripture. One cannot affirm that Christ died for me without first understanding that Christ died.

To establish that Christ died on the cross is a matter of historical evidence. Hence some historical knowledge or confidence in the reporting of the history of Jesus is assumed by saving faith, though such "historical faith" cannot in itself have saving effect or substitute for justifying faith, which believes what it cannot see.

37. FC 37:349.
38. CC, p. 77.

Yet justifying faith does not conclude that historical evidence is unimportant: "We did not follow cleverly invented stories when we told you about the power and coming of our Lord Jesus Christ, but we were eyewitnesses of his majesty" (2 Pet. 1:16; cf. 1 John 1:1ff.).

The proper rules of eyewitnesses were honored. This is seen in the case of the Transfiguration: "We ourselves heard this voice that came from heaven when we were with him on the sacred mountain" (2 Pet. 1:18). Peter was "an eyewitness of Christ's majesty" (2 Pet. 1:16). "Peter says that he has not invented stories like those of the Valentinians but merely handed on the teaching of Christ in simple and humble words, as Paul also told the Corinthians he was doing" (1 Cor. 2:1; Oecumenius, Commentary on 2 Peter).[39] "Peter knew that Jesus received the Father's confirmation from heaven on three different occasions, in his baptism, at his passion and on the mountain. However, this was the one which he himself witnessed" (Theophylact, Commentary on 2 Peter).[40] "This salvation, which was first announced by the Lord, was confirmed to us by those who heard him. God also testified to it by signs, wonders and various miracles, and gifts of the Holy Spirit" (Heb. 2:3, 4).[41]

Saving faith is distinguished from intellectual conviction that arises out of a logical or historical argument. One may be reasonably convinced that God is holy and loving, yet not trust that God in Christ has personally loved him (so as to save "even me," Wesley, JJW, May 24, 1738). It is possible to believe intellectually in the orthodoxy of the doctrine of forgiveness, yet not personally trust God from the heart for the forgiveness of one's own sins. "For it is with your heart that you believe and are justified" (Rom. 10:10).[42] The mouth only confesses rightly what comes deeply from the heart. On these points patristic and Reformed exegetes agree.

D. An Act of Mind, Will, and Heart

Three elements are combined in saving faith: a fully convinced affirmation of the truth of God's self-disclosure; a voluntary surrender of one's will to

39. PG 119:588; ACCS NT 11:139.
40. PG 125:1264; ACCS NT 11:140.
41. Calvin, Comm. XXII, pp. 53-56.
42. Calvin, On Reform, SW, pp. 163-70.

God's will; and a sincere reversal of one's emotive energies, so that all loves are subsumed in relation to the love of God.

The Westminster Confession summed up the "principal acts of saving faith" as "accepting, receiving, and resting upon Christ alone for justification" (Westminster Confession, XIV).[43] This can be schematized as follows:

Assent of the Mind to the Truth of the Word
Consent of the Will to Obey the Word
Trust of the Heart in the Living Word

Thus every act of sincere faith wells up from the whole person as knowing, feeling, and willing (Augustine, Trinity, IX-X).[44]

1. Faith Assents with the Mind to the Truth of the Word

Justifying faith implies and requires belief in the truth, a conviction that what is believed — God's word addressed on the cross — is true and worthy of confidence (Heb. 6:18; Augustine, On the Profit of Believing 34).[45] One cannot be saved by that which is not true.

Saving faith embraces (but is not reducible to) an intellectual aspect, a recognition of the truth of God's self-disclosure. Without the conviction that the history of divine self-disclosure is reliable and reported with sufficient reliability to be believed, faith cannot proceed toward trust and obedience.

This is why careful evidentiary presentation of the facts concerning revelation is a premise of teaching faith and discipleship. If faith is at one level a kind of knowing, then it must be known and taught in the same way that other forms of knowing are known and taught: through accurate data gathering and presentation, logical organization and deduction, and critical rational analysis.

Jesus urged a critical spirit: "If I am not doing the works of my Father, then do not believe me; but if I do them, even though you do not

43. CC, p. 209.
44. NPNF 1 3:125-43.
45. NPNF 1 3:363-64.

believe me, believe the works, that you may know and understand that the Father is in me" (John 10:37, 38; Augustine, Comm. on John, Tractate XLVIII).[46]

Personal trust in Christ strengthens the rigor of Christian intellectual inquiry. Further inquiry strengthens the depth of personal trust. Paul referred to this aspect of faith when he sought to "take captive every thought to make it obedient to Christ" (2 Cor. 10:5). Piety is imperiled when it rejects the intellectual aspect of faith (Clement of Alexandria, Stromata, V.1;[47] Irenaeus, Against Heresies 1[48]).

John's Gospel was written for this specific purpose: "that you may believe *that* Jesus is the Christ, the Son of God, and that by believing you may have life in his name" (John 20:31, italics added). The belief is primarily *in* Jesus personally, but this presupposes *that* Jesus is the Son of God.

"Faith comes from hearing the message, and the message is heard through the word of Christ" (Rom. 10:17). The Word of God speaks in "each particular passage" of scripture in different ways, "yielding obedience to the commands, trembling at the threatenings, and embracing the promises of God" (Westminster Confession, XIV).[49] As adequate evidence is being laid out in preaching, it is hoped that grace is making trust in God possible. Such evidence has been set forth by the Evangelists in the life, death, and resurrection of Jesus.

"Here is a trustworthy saying that deserves full acceptance: Christ Jesus came into the world to save sinners" (1 Tim. 1:15). This statement calls for unfeigned assent to the truth it attests. Yet more than mental assent is required for saving faith. With assent must be joined a personal trust by which one says: these events pertain to me as true for me. So the Apostle immediately adds: "Christ Jesus came into the world to save sinners — of whom I am the worst."

46. NPNF 1 7:266-69.
47. ANF 2:445f.
48. ANF 1:315ff.
49. CC, p. 209.

2. Faith Consents with the Whole Will to Surrender to the Word

The second dimension of faith is the decision of the will. Faith is a radical willing by which the person decisively renounces other gods. Faith is finally an unfettered kind of willing — a willing to trust the incomparably good will of the saving God.

This volitional element of faith is not merely a momentary surrender to God, but an enduring determination to walk daily in accountability toward God.

Although the invitation is offered in principle to all, it is answered only by some. Faith in Christ is therefore a decision. "I stand at the door and knock. If anyone hears my voice and opens the door, I will come in and eat with him, and he with me" (Rev. 3:20). The choice is ours, for "to all who received him, to those who believed in his name, he gave the right to become children of God" (John 1:12).

"Faith is when my heart and the Holy Ghost in the heart says, The promise of God is true and certain" (Apology of the Augsburg Confession).[50] "Faith signifies *assent* to the promise of God, which is in the intellect, and with this assent is necessarily connected *confidence*, which is the will, willing and accepting the promised reconciliation."[51]

3. Faith Trusts with the Heart in the Living Word

Finally, the decisive element of faith is the trust of the heart. Job's trust in God points to the radical character of risk in faith: "Though he slay me, yet will I trust in him" (Job 13:15).

This central element of faith is an act of confidence or unfettered trust (Eph. 3:12; πεποίθησις, Clement of Rome, Cor. 26.1; 35.2).[52] It relies upon what is believed.[53] "Justifying faith implies, not only a Divine evidence or conviction that God was in Christ reconciling the world unto Himself, but a sure trust and confidence that Christ died for *my* sins,

---

50. Sec. 103, p. 122, Jacobs, SCF, p. 188.
51. Melanchthon, CR XXI.790; in SHD II 361.
52. ECW, pp. 37, 41.
53. Chrysostom, Baptismal Instructions, ACW 31:171-72, 245-46.

that He loved me and gave Himself for me" (Wesley, WJWB, I, Sermon V).[54]

In trusting God, faith abandons all competing idolatrous sources of reliance. Faith excludes all other claims of gods that pretend to bestow the final meaning upon life. Faith cleaves only to One worthy of absolute trust, the triune God.

Faith requires the assent of the whole heart, the confident affirmation of the whole person, not of the mind only. Through personal assent, the facts of revelation become graciously applied to one's own personal life and situation.

Faith as trust surrenders the whole mind, heart, and soul to God (Clement of Rome, Cor. 10.1, 11), receiving and appropriating Christ's justifying action and participating in Christ's obedience as the source of pardon and renewal (Luther, On the Councils, LW 41:110-13).[55]

Faith acts from the unifying center of the human person. This is what is signified by the metaphor of the heart. "For it is with your heart that you believe [καρδία γὰρ πιστεύεται] and are justified" (Rom. 10:10).

When the confessor says: "I believe" (πιστεύω, credo), it is an utterance from the heart. The whole person — not just the mind or fleeting feelings — is saying, "I believe."

One may intellectually assent to Christian teaching without personally trusting in the saving work of the Mediator. Lacking personal trust, bare intellectual assent is hardly sufficient for salvation. "You believe that there is one God. Good! Even the demons believe that — and shudder" (James 2:19). Such outward belief is not likely to survive cross-bearing, much less skeptical inquiry.

Luther defined true faith as "that assured trust and firm assent of heart by which Christ is laid hold of."[56] Similarly, the Anglican Homily of Salvation spoke of faith as "a sure trust and confidence in God's merciful promises, to be saved from everlasting damnation by Christ: whereof doth follow a loving heart to obey his commandments."[57] Paul prayed that each believer would be "strengthened in your inner being, so that Christ may dwell in your hearts through faith" (Eph. 3:16, 17).

---

54. WJW, V:53-64.
55. Cf. Calvin, Inst. 3.2; 3.11.
56. Commentary on Luke, in Gamertsfelder, ST, p. 495.
57. A Sermon on the Salvation of Mankind, CC, p. 249.

These three elements are melded in saving faith: a fully convinced affirmation of the truth of God's self-disclosure; a voluntary surrender of
one's will to God's will; and a wholehearted reversal of one's emotive energies, so that all loves are subsumed in relation to the love of God.

Conclusion

What do Christians of all times and places believe about justification by grace through faith? We have set forth the stable, central core. We have meditated on the whole range of the Bible concerning a single theme of it: justification, the heart of the gospel. The three parts of this teaching have a simple organization, based on the key terms of Ephesians 2:8 (viewed in the light of Rom. 3:21-28):

- Salvation
- By Grace
- Through Faith

What have we accomplished? What has the study shown? What is now settled as a result?

Never in the future will it be reasonable, if our evidence is correct, to assume that the patristic writers were ignorant of Paul's justification teaching.

Nothing new, creative, or innovative has been "added on" to "improve" the apostolic teaching of the gospel, but a consensus has been demonstrated as to its generally accepted interpretation.

Now it is clear that Protestants, Catholics, and Orthodox all can appeal to the same authoritative texts on the doctrine of justification by grace through faith, since the earliest authoritative sources (canonical scripture, the ecumenical councils, the key Fathers of East and West) substantially agree on the core of what the apostles taught.

A potentially confusing and often misunderstood central Christian teaching, justification, has been set forth for ordinary lay Christian believers without appealing to technical language.

Once they have grasped this central teaching, everything else in Christianity falls into place more understandably and powerfully.

The same comforting doctrine taught by Paul, the ancient Christian writers, and the Reformers, is stunningly pertinent today to current human problems.

Pre-European texts that are not embarrassing to the two-thirds world of Christians in Africa and Asia may now be appealed to without the baggage of either colonialism or modernity.

The Reformers themselves appealed to the orthodox consensus that preceded them.

The proximate unity of orthodox, consensual Christian teaching in the first five centuries is the most reliable basis for moving beyond the doctrinal divisions and polemics of the last five centuries.

This patristic exercise in some modest ways ratifies and corroborates what once-polarized Lutherans and Catholics have together recently agreed. They have at long last come to understand themselves to be "now able to articulate a common understanding of justification" (JD, Preamble 5), so much so that "remaining differences in its explication are no longer the occasion for doctrinal condemnations" (JD, Preamble 5). While not all parties consent with the same confidence to their Joint Declaration, a point of contact has been found, a chasm has been spanned, a way opened, to make subsequent interactions more charitable.

The major Reformers' appeals to *sola scriptura, sola gratia,* and *sola fide* are found abundantly in the patristic interpreters of scripture.

In this the first of a series of Readers, we have presented a model for integrating classical ecumenical theology, exegetical theology, and systematic theology.

This method can be applied to other controversial issues that divide Christians, such as questions on creation, the human condition, sexuality, intergenerational sin, atonement, the work of the Holy Spirit, charismatic gifts, baptism, ministry, the holy life, and final judgment.

The Holy Spirit appears to be at work in our time to bring diverse believers of many world cultures into greater awareness of the early Christian interpreters of scripture as the most reliable basis for rediscovering our unity in Christ.

Christ's prayer for the unity of believers is being answered once again in remarkable ways by Christians of all sorts — Orthodox, Catholic, mainline Protestant, Evangelical, charismatic, and Pentecostal believers — who are again turning to the classic scriptural interpreters and the plausible consensus they achieved prior to the fragmentations of the second millennium.